JOHNNY REB'S WAR
BATTLEFIELD AND HOMEFRONT

by
David Williams

McWhiney Foundation Press
McMurry University
Abilene, Texas

Cataloging-in-Publication Data

Williams, David, 1959-
Johnny Reb's war: battlefield and homefront / by David Williams
p. cm.
Includes bibliographical references and index.
ISBN 1-893114-23-6 (alk. paper)
1. Soldiers—Confederate States of America—social conditions. 2. Confederate States of America. Army–Military life. 3. Social classes–Confederate States of America–History. 4. Confederate States of America–Social conditions. 5. United States–History–Civil War, 1861-1865–Social aspects. I. Title

E607 .W55 2000
973.7'42–dc21

00-052097
CIP

Box 637, McMurry Station
Abilene, Texas 79697-067

Printed in Abilene, Texas
United States of America

ISBN 1-893114-23-6
10 9 8 7 6 5 4 3 2 1

Book Designed by Rosenbohm Graphic Design

All inquiries regarding volume purchases of this book should be addressed to the McWhiney Foundation Press, Box 637, McMurry Station, Abilene, TX 79697-0637
Telephone inquiries may be made by calling (915) 793-4682

www.mcwhiney.org

To the memory of my great-great-grandfather

John Joseph Kirkland

First Corporal, Company A
51st Georgia Volunteer Infantry Regiment
Army of Northern Virginia

TABLE OF CONTENTS

JOHNNY REB'S WAR
BATTLEFIELD AND HOMEFRONT

INTRODUCTION

"No One Ever Saw a Private"

By the end of August 1862, Confederate General Robert E. Lee's Army of Northern Virginia was in dire need of rest. Since the beginning of the Peninsular Campaign in March of that year, the Johnny Rebs had been fighting, marching, and sustaining casualties at an appalling rate. In late June, they had thrown back the Federal Army of the Potomac, more than 100,000 strong, in a series of battles known as the Seven Days. Then they turned north on a march of nearly 200 miles to Manassas and there routed a 62,000-man Union army in the Second Battle of Manassas. These campaigns had reduced their strength from a force of about 80,000 to just more than 50,000 men.

The killing pace was beginning to tell on this now veteran army. The boys were clothed in little better than rags, thousands were without shoes, and underwear was a luxury. With little rest during the long months of campaigning and a diet of hardly more than salted pork and corn meal, the soldiers had been driven to the verge of collapse. What food they had was nearly gone and most soldiers had to forage in order to feed themselves. The Army of Northern Virginia was in no condition to travel, let alone undertake a campaign of the proportions Lee had in mind. But the time was ripe for a bold thrust northward, and Lee knew it.

On the third of September, three days after his victory at Second Manassas, Lee sent a letter to President Jefferson Davis that announced his intention to enter Maryland. The general outlined his reasoning, but expressed one primary misgiving: "The army is not properly equipped for an invasion of an enemy's territory. It lacks much of the material of war, is feeble in transportation, the animals being much reduced, and the men are poorly provided with clothes, and in thousands of instances are destitute of shoes."[1]

Lee knew that the invasion's success depended mainly on the fortitude of his soldiers. Considering what they had only recently been through, he knew they were reaching the limits of their endurance. How swiftly could they march on the hard, stoney roads of Maryland with their swollen and, in many cases, bleeding feet? How long could they travel on a sparse diet of green corn? How far could they march until they dropped from sheer exhaustion? The future of the Confederacy was at stake and that future rested on the shoulders of Johnny Reb. As Luther Hopkins of Major General J.E.B. Stuart's cavalry put it: "It is the boy who decides the fate of nations. . . . Yet, strange to say, the historian has never thought it worthwhile to put much emphasis upon what the boy does in the upbuilding of a nation."[2]

Many young men recognized that discrepancy. Tennessee Private Sam Watkins reflected the attitude of a great many soldiers, both Reb and Yank, when he wrote after the war, "a private had no right to know anything, and that is why generals did all the fighting. . . . They fought the battles of our country. The privates did not." In that same paragraph he made the poignant observation that "the generals risked their reputation, the private soldier his life. No one ever saw a private in battle."[3]

Even more obscure were the homefront factors that had such an impact on the battlefield. Though more has been written on the Civil War era than any other period in American history, most of that literature deals with its military aspects. But Johnny Reb was not a single-

Confederate General Robert E. Lee, Library of Congress.

minded killing machine with no thought but to shoot Yankees. In most cases, he had a family back home. Their worries were his too. When they suffered, he suffered. And when he asked himself why they were suffering and what he could do to ease their pain, the conclusions he reached usually did not meet with his generals' approval.

The following pages, drawn mainly from first-hand accounts, represent an effort to follow that soldier known as Johnny Reb on the battlefield and homefront, to consider how the hardships that he and his family endured shaped their attitudes, and to understand how those attitudes affected the war's outcome.

NOTES

1. United States War Department, *War of the Rebellion: A Compilation of the Official Records of the Union and Confederate Armies*, 128 parts in 70 vols. and atlas (Washington, D.C.: Government Printing Office, 1880-1901), series. 1, vol. 19, part 2, p. 590. Hereafter cited as *O.R.*

2. Luther Hopkins, *From Bull Run to Appomattox: A Boy's View* (Baltimore: Fleet-McGinley, 1914), 4.

3. Sam R. Watkins, *Co. Aytch* (New York: Macmillan Publishing, 1962), 66.

BATTLEFIELD: THE CRUCIBLE OF SHARPSBURG

"Bleeding Feet"

Nearly half a century after the distant September campaign of 1862, one Southerner recalled the sad condition of the Army of Northern Virginia: "The lack of shoes was deplorable, and barefooted men with bleeding feet were no uncommon sight. Of clothing, our supply was so poor that it seemed no wonder the Marylanders held aloof from our shabby ranks. For rations, we were indebted mostly to the fields of roasting ears and to the apple orchards."[1] Old soldiers often exaggerate when they reminiscence about events that in later years become the focus of their lives—but not in this case. If anything, the description falls far short of painting a clear portrait of the misery and privation suffered by Johnny Reb between the time he set out for Maryland on September 1, 1862, and the nineteenth day of that month when he returned to Virginia after the bloody Battle of Sharpsburg—or, as the Federals called it, Antietam.

Of the roughly 50,000 men left to Lee after the Second Battle of Manassas, perhaps 40,000 needed shoes.[2] This situation reflected a much larger problem that had plagued the Confederacy since the

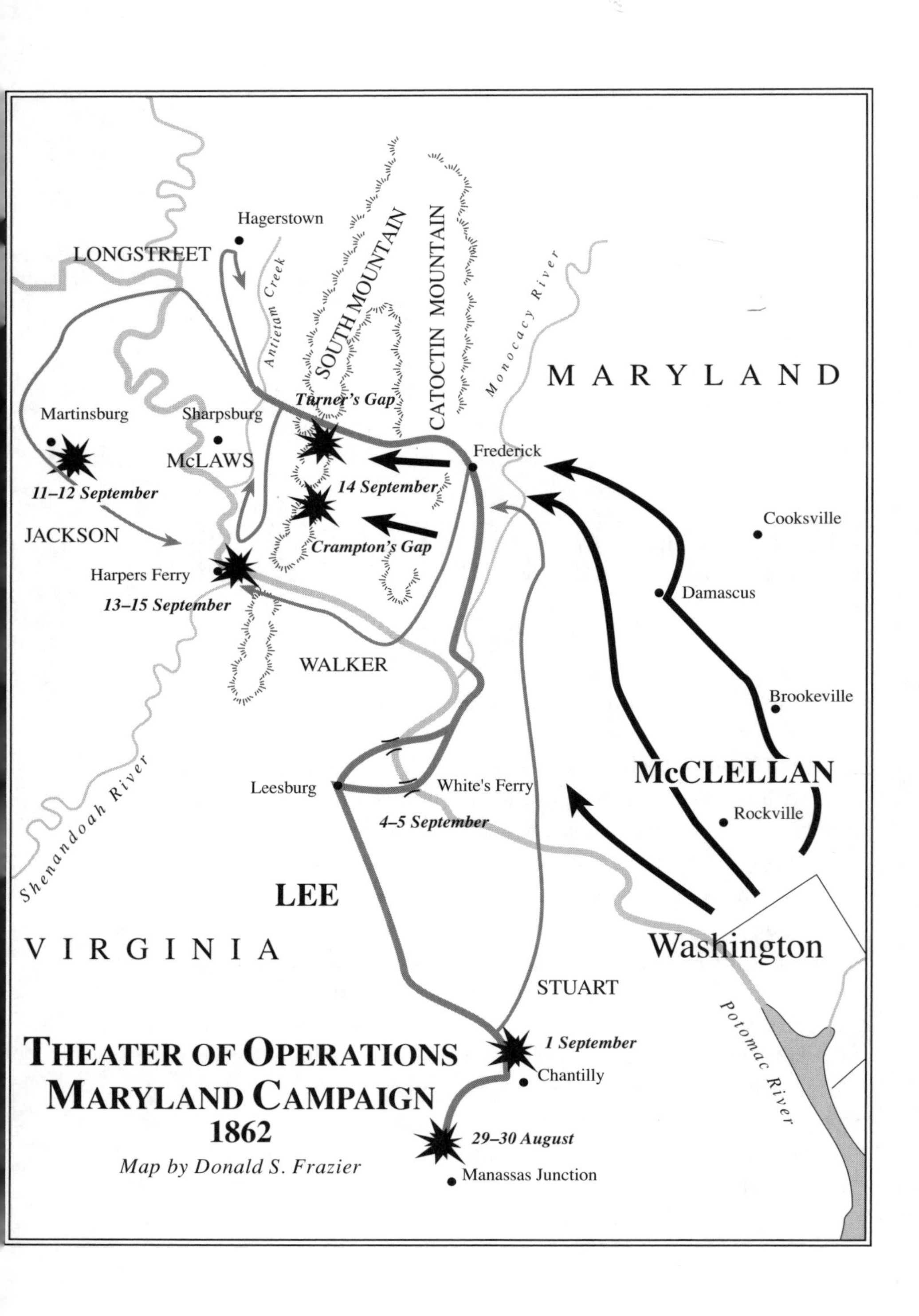
Hagerstown
LONGSTREET
Antietam Creek
SOUTH MOUNTAIN
CATOCTIN MOUNTAIN
Monocacy River
MARYLAND
Turner's Gap
Martinsburg
Sharpsburg
McLAWS
Frederick
14 September
11–12 September
JACKSON
Crampton's Gap
Cooksville
Harpers Ferry
13–15 September
Damascus
WALKER
Brookeville
Shenandoah River
McCLELLAN
Leesburg
White's Ferry
4–5 September
Rockville
LEE
VIRGINIA
Washington
STUART
Potomac River
THEATER OF OPERATIONS
MARYLAND CAMPAIGN
1862
Map by Donald S. Frazier
1 September
Chantilly
29–30 August
Manassas Junction

war's beginning. Raw leather was scarce in the South because Southerners were used to buying leather goods from northern factories. The only source of leather available to the South after secession had been the cattle and horse farms and the fledgling tanneries of Tennessee. But the Union invasion of that state in the spring of 1862 had cut off even this meager source. By September, after a summer of almost constant marching, nearly all of Lee's men had worn out their shoes, and the Confederacy found it difficult to supply them with new ones. Most of what shoes the army possessed had been removed from the feet of the dead as they lay rotting on the Manassas battlefield. John Worsham of Major General Thomas J. "Stonewall" Jackson's "Foot Cavalry" reported that of the hundreds of dead Yankees he saw, not one was wearing a pair of shoes.[3] Nor did the feet of deceased Rebels escape plunder. Private George Bernard remembered in his memoirs that after the battle there was "a very general removing of shoes, not only from the Federal dead, but also from many of the dead Confederates."[4]

Though the need for footgear among Southerners was great, there were those who simply could not bring themselves to plunder a lifeless corpse. Private Bernard counted himself one of this number after a vain attempt to overcome his anxiety.

> I went to this poor fellow's feet, untied one of his shoes and began to pull it off. This was, of course, not easy work, and whilst engaged at it I suddenly fully realized what I was doing—taking a dead man's shoes, and these the shoes of a dead Confederate! I at once stopped, and swore I would go bare-footed before would do an act which was so repugnant to my feelings.[5]

For those not so disinclined, there were other hazards involved in the search for shoes. Straggling and desertion became severe problems in the army, with equally severe punishments for men accused of these transgressions. Soldiers straying from the ranks to secure footwear might easily be taken for deserters, swollen or bleeding feet notwithstanding.

One such incident occurred shortly after Second Manassas. It involved a sergeant of the 16th Mississippi Infantry Regiment, who had set out alone to procure a pair of shoes from among the dead. While on his way back to his unit, the young sergeant spotted a small group of men on horseback headed his way. As they drew nearer, one of the horsemen approached and asked what the sergeant was doing away from his command. When he replied, "That's none of your business, by God," he immediately was accused of being a straggler. Unwilling to allow this insult to go unchallenged, the soldier snapped, "It's a damned lie, sir! I only left my regiment a few minutes ago to hunt me a pair of shoes. I went through all the fight yesterday, and that's more than you can say: for where were you yesterday when General Stuart wanted your damned cavalry to charge the Yankees after we put 'em to running? You were lying back in the pine thickets and couldn't be found; but today, when there's no danger, you come out and charge other men with straggling, damn you." Somewhat taken aback by this display of grit, the horseman paused for an instant and then burst into laughter. As the group turned to continue on its way, one of the riders asked the feisty sergeant if he knew to whom he had just spoken. Of course he knew—"a cowardly Virginia cavalryman." The young man no doubt was shocked to learn the identity of his accuser—General Robert E. Lee.[6]

For those in the Southern army who found it impossible to obtain shoes, the march from Manassas to Leesburg was fairly easy going because of the soft, dusty dirt roads of Virginia's piedmont. But the situation changed dramatically after the army crossed the Potomac several miles north of Leesburg. At White's Ford, where most of the army began crossing into Maryland on September 4, the rocky bottom of the river cut and bruised unprotected feet. Worse yet, the roads of western Maryland were hard and rocky, and many a good soldier found it impossible to keep pace.

By the time Lee's troops had assembled at Sharpsburg, thousands were absent because their feet simply could not carry them to the battlefield. Even so, there were thousands more of the unshod who did participate in the fighting along the banks of Antietam Creek. Heros von Borcke, chief of J.E.B. Stuart's staff, remembered that "it was astonishing to see men without shoes, whose lacerated feet often stained their path with blood, limping to the front."[7]

Others, however, literally could not go the extra mile. Among those who found that there were limits to what human feet could endure was a tall farmer from the mountains of northern Georgia. When he finally caught up with his unit after the battle, his commanding officer demanded to know the reason for his absence. Striking a tone of undeniable logic, the lanky Georgian replied: "I had no shoes. I tried it barefoot, but somehow my feet wouldn't callous. They just kept bleeding. I found it so hard to keep up that though I had the heart of a patriot, I began to feel I didn't have patriotic feet."[8]

"The Dirtiest Men I Ever Saw"

If footwear among the troops left much to be desired, the condition of other garments, and that of the soldiers' very bodies, was hardly any better. An elderly Virginia woman said of the southerners, "they were the dirtiest men I ever saw, a most ragged, lean, and hungry set of wolves."[9] Said another, "There is not a scarecrow in our cornfields that would not scorn to exchange clothes with them."[10]

Most soldiers counted themselves fortunate even to have a decent shirt and a good pair of pants. One former Confederate remembered in later years that he did not believe there was a single shred of underclothing in the entire army.[11] A *Harper's Weekly* correspondent wrote of the Rebel garb: "With the exception of the officers, there was little else but homespun among them, light drab-gray or butternut color, the drab predominating; although there were so many varieties of dress, half citizen, half military that they could scarcely be said to have a uniform.[12]

Aside from the lack of adequate clothing, there was also the problem of cleanliness, or rather the absence of it. One Maryland woman wrote of the Southerners, "Oh, they are so dirty! I don't think the Potomac River could wash them clean."[13] The clouds of dust stirred up by the marching columns caked layer upon layer of filth on the already dirty faces. One soldier, commenting on the movement from Leesburg to White's Ford, said that the dust was so thick, it was impossible to discern a man three yards distant.[14] Another young Rebel proposed "to drill holes through the dirt on some of the boys' faces and blast it off, as water is thought to be inadequate to the task."[15]

Still another soldier related an amusing incident that occurred after the fall of Harpers Ferry two days before the Battle of Sharpsburg. Lee had sent Stonewall Jackson's Corps to capture the Federal garrison at Harpers Ferry, located at the mouth of the valley where the Shenandoah River flows into the Potomac, because he proposed to use the Shenandoah Valley as his supply line during the campaign. The Rebel troops, having been in the field all summer, had deeply tanned skin and were unused to seeing soldiers of light complexion such as those of the Federal garrison.

> As we Marched along the street one of our troopers sang out to one of the men on the sidewalk, "I say, Yank, what sort of soap do you fellows use? It has washed all the color out of your faces," at which our side cheered. To this the man retorted, "Damn me, if you don't look like you have never used soap of any sort." Shouts of laughter greeted the reply from our men as well as the Yanks, and our man called back as he rode on, "Bully for you, Yank; you got me that time."[16]

As if the dirt that caked their bodies was not sufficient to make each soldier feel as if he might never be clean again, there was the additional aggravation of body lice or, as they were called by the troops, "graybacks." For the unfortunate boy who discovered that these annoying creatures had taken up residence on his person there was but one consolation—every man in the army had them.[17]

Body lice infected Lee's entire force, and there appeared to be nothing anyone could do about it. Even so, attempts to get rid of the critters became a constant preoccupation. One favorite pastime among the troops was to exterminate these pests one by one, an activity in which the soldiers seemed to engage "With a vengeful pleasure." One Southern private wrote that, "Every evening in Maryland when the army halted and bivouacked for the night, hundreds of the soldiers could be seen sitting on the roads or fields, half denuded, with their clothes in their laps, busily cracking, between the two thumb-nails, these creeping nuisances."[18] But the effort was in vain for within a day or two the boys found that they were once again "lousy."

"The Green Corn Campaign"

Aside from the lack of proper clothing and cleanliness, soldiers experienced the more pressing concern for food. One of the primary objectives of Lee's Maryland Campaign was to win the state's inhabitants to the Southern cause and gather new recruits for the Rebel forces. To facilitate this process of wooing the Marylanders, Lee issued strict orders against foraging, insisting that the army pay for what it needed. Such a policy was necessary from a political standpoint, but among the rank and file, more often than not, hunger took precedence over political considerations. And the Army of Northern Virginia was very hungry. "They were half famished and they looked like tramps," recalled one Sharpsburg woman, "They nearly worried us to death asking for something to eat."[19] Another woman felt that words were not adequate to express the sad condition of the soldiers. "When I say that they were hungry, I convey no impression of the gaunt starvation that looked from their cavernous eyes."[20]

Despite the fact that hunger most often forced the issue, some Southerners nevertheless could not comprehend why the Maryland countryside should not be plundered. Private John Dooley expressed the prevalent attitude among Confederate troops: "our men having been witnesses of the devastation of fields through the entire state of Virginia, refused to understand why we should spare the fields of those who, if they were not actually hostile themselves, were supporting a hostile government."[21]

The contrast between barren fields of northern Virginia and lush Maryland countryside appeared indeed remarkable. When the Rebels crossed the Potomac, they entered an unfamiliar world, one teeming with orchards of peaches, pears, and apples. Fields of green corn

Despite the South's reputation for agricultural productivity, planters grew so much cotton that there was little food for the army. What food the soldiers had they usually got for themselves. During the Sharpsburg Campaign they foraged so much from farmers' cornfields that one Johnny Reb remembered it years later as "the green corn campaign." Buel and Johnson, Battles and Leaders.

abounded. Since the Confederate commissary system had "about broken down,"[22] officers were authorized to purchase entire fields and orchards from local farmers. But such a starchy and sporadic diet for men who were undernourished to begin with was hardly sufficient to sustain them on a prolonged and rapid march. According to one staff officer, straggling was caused primarily by a lack of food.[23] Furthermore, as a result of the almost exclusive consumption of salted, parched, and boiled corn in many units, attacks of diarrhea escalated to near epidemic proportions. So reliant were the soldiers on this grain that years later one old veteran commented, "We call this even now the green corn campaign."[24]

Although relatively plentiful, fruits and vegetables were not always at hand and even when they were the men needed a supplement of protein. The most readily available source of this nutritional necessity being the fields and barnyards of Maryland farmers, Lee's efforts to restrain foraging proved largely unsuccessful. Southern boys made many a good meal of illegally procured livestock. The standard excuse for such breeches of policy held that the poor soldier had been attacked viciously by some crazed farm animal, and the threatened man had no choice but to shoot the creature. Recalled one member of Stuart's Horse Artillery, "Some of the men came into camp one morning with a pig, and declared that the pig attacked them, and they were obliged to kill it in self defense. It was keenly enjoyed for breakfast and no questions asked."[25]

An even less plausible excuse made the rounds in Sharpsburg the day after the battle. As many dislocated farm animals wandered the streets, famished Southerners, taking pity on the "poor little things," did not hesitate to put them out of their homeless misery. One soldier explained, "They have nowhere to go and we ought to take care of them."[26]

Occasionally, the "innocent victim" of a purported livestock assault got caught in the act by an officer inclined to see Lee's orders carried out. Major von Borcke recalled one such incident. Although von Borcke understood that the army had been subsisting on little more than apples and green corn for weeks, he nonetheless . . .

> felt obliged to rebuke a Texan, who, only a few steps from me, had just rolled over, by a capital shot, a porker galloping across the street at sixty yards distance, for his wanton disregard of the rights of property. With a look of utter astonishment, he turned to me, and asked, "Major, did you have anything to eat yesterday?" and, upon my answering in the negative, said, "Then you know what it is to be hungry; I haven't tasted a morsel for several days." I had nothing more to say, and mounting my horse, I rode forward to the front.[27]

Another incident concerning a Sharpsburg "porker" involved none other than Lee himself. By all accounts, Lee was man who usually kept himself under control. One of his aides remembered that, to his knowledge, only twice did the general allow a hint of temper to crack his normally calm exterior. Apparently, the stress of battle at

Sharpsburg was sufficient to bring on one outburst. As Lee passed along the rear of his battle line, he came across a young soldier who, like so many before him, had been "assaulted" by a pig and was preparing to make a meal of the animal. Lee was outraged at this blatant violation of his orders and determined to make an example of the would-be pork thief. Although usually not inclined to employ capital punishment, Lee sent the young man, a member of Jackson's Corps, to "Old Stonewall" with orders to have him shot. This young Southerner must have been sure that he had seen his last sunrise, but when presented to Jackson for execution, the general felt that since the army was so short of men, it would be a waste to shoot the soldier outright. Instead, Jackson proposed to let the Yankees carry out this particular order for him, and placed the young man at a position on the front line, where the fighting was heaviest. While willing to disobey orders to satisfy hunger, this fellow was no coward. He performed admirably under fire and went through the day without so much as a scratch. Wrote one of Lee's aides concerning the young soldier, "If a commonplace witticism be not out of place here, it may be said that, though he lost his pig, he 'saved his bacon.'"[28]

"Our Ranks Are Very Much Diminished"

Lack of food, along with inadequate supplies of footwear, resulted in a critical depletion of manpower as the army moved through Frederick and into western Maryland. On September 13, Lee wrote to Jefferson Davis from Hagerstown: "One great embarrassment is the reduction of our ranks by straggling, which it seems impossible to prevent with our present regimental officers. Our ranks are very much diminished, I fear from a third to a half of the original numbers."[29]

Regardless of the exact count, it was clear that thousands of hungry, tired, and footsore soldiers were unable to keep up with the army. According to one artilleryman in Major General James Longstreet's Corps, "Brigades were often reduced to the size of regiments, and regiments to the size of companies."[30]

In addition to the problem of hunger and lack of shoes, a chief cause of straggling was quite simply the grueling pace of the march. Key to Lee's strategy for a successful invasion of the North was rapid movement. He knew Major General George McClellan, commanding the Army of the Potomac, to be a cautious man and hoped to take advantage of this by literally outrunning him. So the soldiers had to move rapidly. Sometimes they marched deep into the night, with only two or three hours sleep; sometimes they marched throughout the night, with no sleep at all. One weary soldier wrote in his journal that "it looked to a man in the ranks as if our officers supposed we were not ordinary flesh and blood."[31]

The things that the human body can endure and adapt to are without doubt amazing to behold but horrible to experience. At hardly any other time are there more examples of such feats of human endurance than during time of war, when men are pushed to their physical limits. In his diary, John Dooley wrote of his first evening on the march in Maryland: "When night shut out the angry glare [of the sun] we are still marching slowly but wearily along the Maryland roads, sometimes half asleep, sometimes sound asleep. Even when half asleep I moved for miles, my bruised, stiffened limbs mechanically following one the other."[32]

At times during the Maryland Campaign, the pace of march became so exhausting that men singularly or, more commonly, in small groups decided that the time had come for some sleep, and took the initiative in pursuit of slumber. Four young friends did just that on their first night in Maryland. Since the onset of dusk, they had carefully watched the head of the column for any signs of halting for the night, but hour after hour passed with no such indication. Finally, the four decided to break ranks, get some sleep, and catch up to their unit in the morning. They found a comfortable haystack several yards from the road and settled down for some much needed rest. Minutes later, one of the boys noticed signs of the army making camp a few miles up the road and suggested that it might be wise to rejoin their regiment. One of the more exhausted members of the group immediately spoke out against this proposal. "No, no I would not move from this comfortable place, as tired as I am, if my great-grandmother were up there at those fires." The others agreed and all four remained where they were for a good night's sleep. Such opportunities to "hit the hay" (quite literally in this case) would be few.[33]

The problem of straggling was not unexpected in the Army of Northern Virginia. Lee anticipated that straggling would be particularly acute considering the condition of his army after Second Manassas and made provisions to deal with the situation. His first step was to leave a contingent of cavalry on the Virginia side of the Potomac to prevent the already large number of stragglers from following the army into Maryland. Lee felt they would be easily captured by the pursuing Federals and had them diverted to Winchester in the Shenandoah Valley. So great was the number of soldiers who, even at this point, could not keep up with the army that it took nearly a week to route the stragglers toward Winchester.[34]

Even though Winchester was the designated rally point for the army's stragglers, not all arrived accordingly. Many were too ill to travel and remained with families in and around Leesburg for the time being. Others refused to participate in the advance into Maryland, arguing that they had joined the army to defend their homeland, not invade someone else's. Still others, like Private Berry Benson of Georgia, tried to rejoin their regiments despite orders to the contrary. Berry had fallen ill after Second Manassas and was too weak to accompany Jackson's Corps into Maryland. He spent a few days recuperating in the home of a Judge Gray near Leesburg, and then set out in the direction of Winchester. He soon learned that Jackson's Corps was at Harpers Ferry and determined to rejoin his comrades there rather than face the humiliation of the "stragglers' camp."

> Just before reaching Harper's Ferry, I ran into a net. A soldier suddenly stepped out from a gateway and halted me. Though I expostulated, he said he must obey orders to stop all on the road and bring them into the stragglers' camp, to be distributed to their respective commands. Once in, I thought of nothing but how to get out. Sauntering down amongst the wagons parked close to the fence enclosing the grove, I watched my chance for a guard to turn his back,

> then I leaped the fence, ran through the high corn and got away. In an hour I was with the boys, who declared themselves powerful glad to see me again, and gave a full account of the battle of Harper's Ferry.[35]

The manpower drain caused by straggling escalated as the campaign wore on. Consequently, Lee issued strict orders that anyone leaving his place in the column was to be rounded up and returned to his unit immediately. Jackson went even further, stating that any soldier in his corps who broke ranks without a good reason would be shot.[36]

The cavalry was charged with the task of rounding up stragglers and getting them back into line. This was not easy since many of the less enthusiastic boys hid themselves among genuinely ill soldiers. Nevertheless, the work of encouraging the faint hearted continued. As one zealous horseman recalled, "There was great straggling to the rear . . . and [we made] sharp play with the flats of our swords on the backs of these fellows."[37]

Bruised and bloody feet, empty bellies, and plain exhaustion created a shadow army of stragglers that numbered perhaps twenty thousand. Still, the outcome at Sharpsburg most likely would not have been significantly different even if a large fraction of these men had been available for battle on September 17, since the Confederates would have remained outnumbered by as many as forty thousand men. But, as Lee demonstrated on several occasions, numbers did not automatically translate into victory or defeat. In any case, he clearly viewed straggling and desertion as the army's most serious problem.[38]

"Damn My Maryland"

A great majority of Virginians were mighty glad to be rid of the Yankees after Second Manassas and showered their appreciation on the soldiers of Lee's army. James Dinkins of Mississippi recalled that the people of Leesburg "were delighted to see us, and filled our haversacks with 'grub.'"[39] Robert Healy of the 55th Virginia remembered, "The day before the corps waded the Potomac at White's Ford, they marched through Leesburg, where an old lady with upraised hands, and with tears in her eyes exclaimed 'The Lord bless your dirty ragged souls.'"[40] Apparently, the Confederates expected nearly the same sort of welcome from the inhabitants of Maryland. Southerners tended to view Maryland as a sister state held in the Union by force of arms, and that if given the opportunity she would rally to the banner of Southern independence. Lee intended to give Maryland that opportunity.

As the army splashed its way across the Potomac River, regimental bands struck up the pro-Confederate melody "Maryland, My Maryland" in anticipation that the young men of the state would fill the depleted ranks of the Rebel army. Subsequent events, however, proved this expectation to be overly optimistic.

On September 8, as the Army of Northern Virginia camped outside Frederick, Lee issued a proclamation addressed to the people of Maryland in which he promised assistance "to enable you again to enjoy the inalienable rights of freemen and restore independence and sovereignty to your State."[41] But the situation was not quite so simple. Opinion in the central region of Maryland was almost evenly divided on the issue of secession, and the city of Frederick epitomized this division. Even so, many citizens greeted the Confederates with "the liveliest enthusiasm." One soldier wrote of the scene he witnessed in Frederick: "Flags were floating from the houses, and garlands of flowers were hung across the streets. Everywhere a dense multitude was moving up and down, singing and shouting in a paroxysm of joy and patriotic emotion."[42]

Many citizens of Frederick who demonstrated pro-Confederate sentiments were quite sincere in their display of support for the Southerners. But John Dooley recalled that "it was not difficult to discern that this enthusiasm was roused only for the display, and that the large majority of the people were silent in regard to giving demonstrations of opinion: many because they were really hostile to us, and some because they knew that everyone was narrowly watched by Spies, by the remnant of Yankee forces on parole in the town, and most of all by their own neighbors."[43]

As the army continued its march through the passes of South Mountain and into western Maryland, it progressively found little such division of opinion. Almost to a man, sentiment ran strongly in favor of the Union. One young Reb remembered the reception Confederates received in this area of the state as being "sour as vinegar."[44] Jackson himself recognized the contempt of Middletown citizens when he remarked to his staff, "We evidently have no friends in this town."[45]

Often, the people showed their low regard for the ragged Confederates by making unfriendly gestures or by displaying the "Stars and Stripes." William Owen recalled one young woman standing on her front porch who had pinned a small U.S. flag to her blouse. Noticing this badge of defiance, one soldier called out, "Look h'yar, miss; better take that flag down; we're awful fond of charging breastworks!"[46]

Sometimes the natives expressed their sentiments in more direct ways. During the withdrawal of Major General D.H. Hill's Division through Boonsboro after the delaying action at South Mountain, the Rebels took fire not only from the Federals but also from the town's citizens.[47] At Sharpsburg, a farmer broke the handle off his pump to deny fresh water to the Confederates, who were forced to fill their canteens from a mud hole in the farmer's stable lot.[48]

On September 24, one week after the Battle of Sharpsburg, a correspondent of the *Memphis Appeal* wrote to his paper, "Maryland had a few noble patriots in her limits, but as a State, she resembles Ephraim—she is tied to her idol, the g-l-o-r-i-o-u-s Union, and ought to be let alone."[49] By all accounts most of Lee's soldiers felt the same way. Only three weeks before, these boys had waded across the Potomac singing "She breathes, she burns, she'll come, she'll come, Maryland, My Maryland." But she did not come. The total number of Maryland's sons who joined the Confederates in their sweep through the state was probably not more than two hundred.[50] In remembering the retreat and the melody "Maryland, My Maryland," one soldier remarked, "Occasionally some fellow would strike up that tune, and you would then hear the echo, 'Damn My Maryland.'"[51]

"Antietam Creek Ran Red"

Thomas Jefferson Rushin of the 12th Georgia Infantry Regiment was twenty-five years old in September of 1862, yet he was among the elder members of the Army of Northern Virginia. Most were only boys in their late teens. He had been born to Elizabeth and Joel Rushin near Buena Vista, Georgia, about 30 miles east of Columbus. The Rushins lived on a farm in Marion County and enjoyed the bountiful affections of a large family. There were eight children, of which Thomas was the second eldest.[52]

More representative of the Southern soldiers' average age was nineteen-year-old Henry Thomas Davenport, also of the 12th Georgia. He was born to Henry and Julia Rhymes Davenport of Americus and Plains of Dura (later Plains), Georgia, on April 26, 1843.[53] Although separated slightly by age and distance, the current of time would carry both Thomas Rushin and Henry Davenport, along with nearly 130,000 other young men of the North and South, to a fateful September rendezvous on the banks of Antietam Creek.[54]

It was now the evening of September 16, 1862, and the 12th Georgia was positioned in line of battle about a mile north of a small, picturesque village called Sharpsburg, nestled in the valley of the Antietam.[55] The regiment, part of Stonewall Jackson's Corps, had just arrived from Harpers Ferry after capturing the Yankee garrison there.

Lee originally had sent Longstreet's Corps on to Hagerstown to await Jackson's arrival. From there, with his rear secured, he had planned to launch an invasion of Pennsylvania. But after finding a lost copy of Lee's order to divide his army, General McClellan moved to position his Army of the Potomac between the two Confederate corps. Lee quickly drew Longstreet back from Hagerstown, fought a delaying action at South Mountain, and assembled his forces behind Antietam Creek. Leaving Major General A.P. Hill's Division at Harpers Ferry to "mop up," with orders to join him as soon as possible, Jackson rushed to join Lee and Longstreet. After a seventeen-mile forced march, Jackson's men, including those of the 12th Georgia, arrived, tired and hungry, at Sharpsburg.

Despite their exhaustion, sleep did not come easily to many sol-

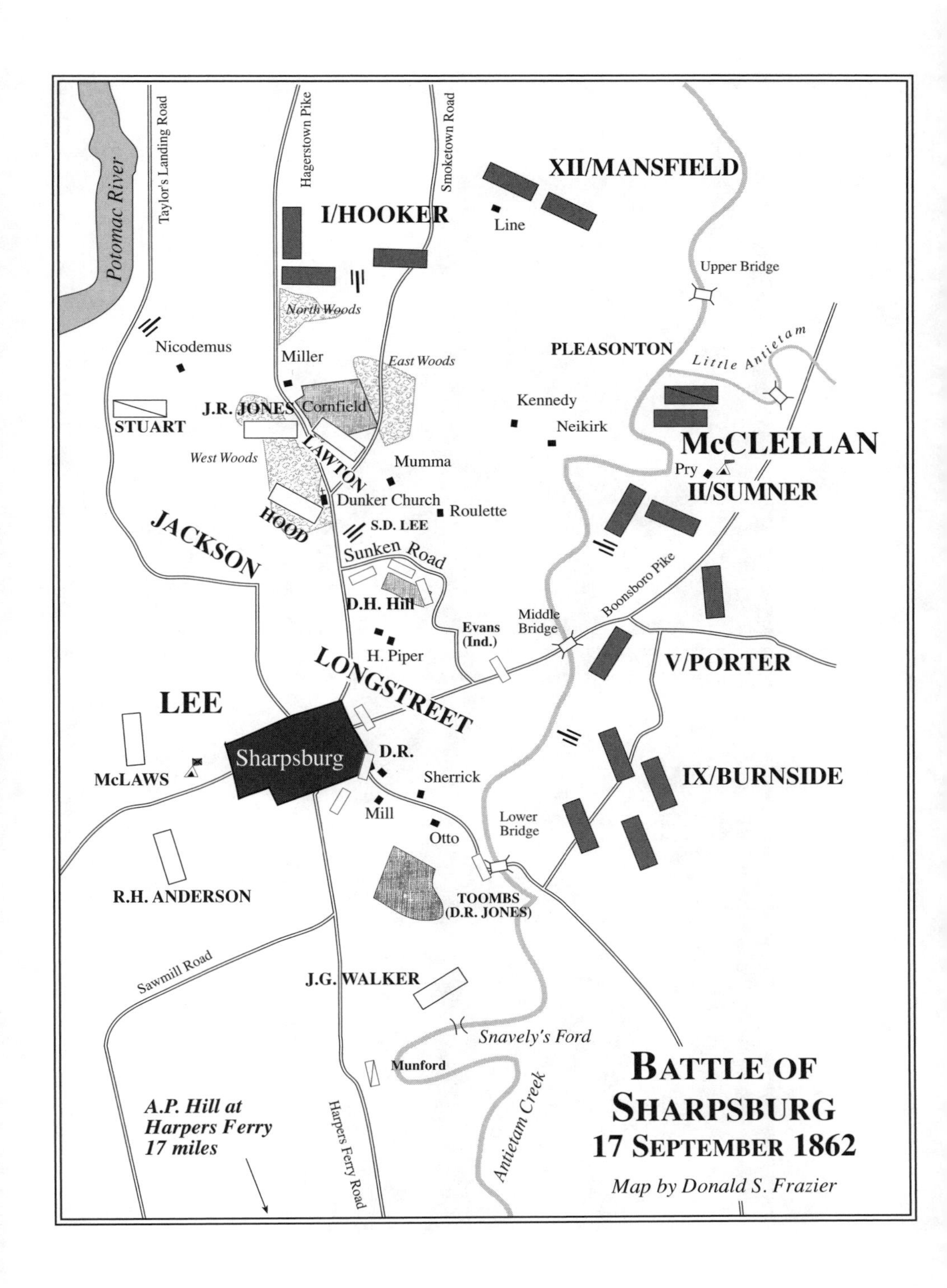
Potomac River
Taylor's Landing Road
Hagerstown Pike
Smoketown Road
XII/MANSFIELD
I/HOOKER
Line
Upper Bridge
North Woods
Nicodemus
Miller
East Woods
PLEASONTON
Little Antietam
Kennedy
J.R. JONES
Cornfield
STUART
Neikirk
LAWTON
McCLELLAN
West Woods
Mumma
Pry
II/SUMNER
Dunker Church
Roulette
JACKSON
HOOD
S.D. LEE
Sunken Road
Boonsboro Pike
D.H. Hill
Middle Bridge
Evans (Ind.)
H. Piper
V/PORTER
LONGSTREET
LEE
Sharpsburg
D.R.
McLAWS
Sherrick
IX/BURNSIDE
Mill
Lower Bridge
Otto
R.H. ANDERSON
TOOMBS (D.R. JONES)
Sawmill Road
J.G. WALKER
Snavely's Ford
Munford
A.P. Hill at Harpers Ferry 17 miles
Harpers Ferry Road
Antietam Creek
BATTLE OF SHARPSBURG
17 SEPTEMBER 1862
Map by Donald S. Frazier

Sergeant Thomas Jefferson Rushin (top) and Private Henry Thomas Davenport of the 12th Georgia Infantry. Both were from southwest Georgia and had enlisted early in the war. Their regiment was among the first to see action that day. One would not survive the battle. The other barely survived the war. Georgia Department of Archives and History; University of Georgia Libraries.

Just after daybreak, soldiers of the Major General Joseph Hooker's Federal I Corps crashed out of the East Woods and the Cornfield, touching off fighting in what would become the bloodiest day in American history. Buel and Johnson, Battles and Leaders.

diers of the 12th Georgia that night. They understood, as did the men of both armies, that the coming dawn would bring death for thousands. Most tried not to dwell too much on the thought of death. There were casualties in every battle, but the majority escaped injury and each man counted the chances good that he might be among the more fortunate. With this thought, most of the soldiers tried to get some sleep. They knew that they would need it for the coming day.

As the long night wore on, a drizzling rain began to fall, which compounded the miserable conditions and increased tension all along the line. Some of the pickets grew so jumpy that they began to shoot at anything that moved. Occasionally, the sporadic firing became so intense that a night attack seemed imminent.[56] But no such attack came, and the long wait for dawn continued.

First light on the seventeenth found the 12th Georgia in an open field south of Smoketown Road just northwest of Samuel Mumma's farm house. Two hundred yards directly in front of the regiment was a patch of timber known as the East Woods, which had been occupied by Federals the night before. About five hundred yards to the west, the men could see a small white building, the Dunker Church, highlighted against the background of the West Woods. Another five hundred yards to the north was a cornfield, forever after known as *the* Cornfield, stretching from the East Woods to the Hagerstown Turnpike.

The rain had stopped by now and a foggy mist hung low and heavy over the field. Thomas Rushin, Henry Davenport, and the other

This image of Rebel dead along Hagerstown Turnpike taken two days after the battle attests to the ferocity of combat at this point of the line. Library of Congress.

Dunker Church, seen here a few days after the battle. Confederate dead of Colonel Stephen D. Lee's artillery battalion lie in the foreground. Library of Congress.

men of the 12th Georgia were hungry, and their homespun clothing was damp and itchy. But there was no time to think of comfort. The boys could do no more than lie on the cold, wet ground and wait for the Yankee attack. It was not long in coming.

As soon as it was light enough to see, the Southerners on Mumma's farm were startled by the thunder of cannon off to the east, across Antietam Creek. The boys tightened their grips on the rifles they carried, and strained in the hazy dawn light to see several Rebel pickets running toward them from the direction of the East Woods. An instant later the flame and smoke of musketry erupted along the tree line and hot lead tore through the regiment. Some of the boys

The burned out buildings of the Mumma farm as they appeared a few days after the battle. The 12th Georgia and later the 4th Georgia had been stationed not far beyond the tree on the left. The East Woods can be seen in the distance on the right. Library of Congress.

crouched low in the loose dirt; others took cover behind tombstones in the Mumma family cemetery. The 12th Georgia, along with the other regiments of Colonel James A. Walker's Brigade (A.R. Lawton's Division), prepared their muzzle-loaders for return fire.

The entire Yankee line facing Walker's Brigade was concealed in the East Woods, except for a section that opposed his left, where the 12th Georgia was positioned. In his official report, Walker recorded events of the next few minutes:

> Observing that the cool and deliberate fire of this tried and veteran regiment [the 12th Georgia] was annoying that portion of the enemy's line very greatly, I ordered the Twenty-first Georgia and Twenty-first North Carolina Regiments to the left, taking shelter under a low stone fence running at right angles to their former line, to direct their fire upon the wavering Yankee regiment, with the view of breaking the enemy's line at this point. They did so promptly, and a few rounds from them had the desired effect and the enemy's line was entirely broken.[57]

The Rebels now held the initiative in this part of the field. With newly arrived units supporting his left, Walker ordered the brigade forward. It had advanced only a short distance when the support troops, under heavy fire, began to break and run. Walker's left flank was now fully exposed. He had little choice but to order his men back to the stone fence. Here Walker held his ground, but he knew he could not hold the position for long. The brigade had suffered heavy casualties, and ammunition was running so low that the boys were gathering cartridges from their fallen comrades.

At about 6:45 a.m., just as the brigade began to falter, orders came to withdraw, and fresh troops moved up to fill the gap. The 12th Georgia, along with the rest of Walker's Brigade, made its way to the rear of Sharpsburg, where it was held in reserve. But the brigade had suffered casualties enough to make it useless for the rest the day. The 12th Georgia alone had gone into battle with more than a hundred men. Fewer than fifty remained.

The news was little better along other parts of the Rebel line. As Walker's Brigade pulled back, Brigadier General John Bell Hood's Division was being driven out of the Cornfield, across Hagerstown Pike, and through the West Woods by Major General Joseph Hooker's I Corps. After suffering heavy losses, Hood's men finally reformed and held fast behind the West Woods. Later that morning, just to the south, D. H. Hill's Confederates were driven back across Hagerstown Pike by Major General Edwin V. Sumner's II Corps, after putting up stiff resistance along Bloody Lane. Had McClellan thrown his reserve corps under Major General Fitz John Porter into the battle at that point, he almost surely would have broken Lee's line.

McClellan had another opportunity to use his reserve corps decisively that afternoon, when Ambrose Burnside's IX Corps crossed Antietam Creek and drove Longstreet's men back toward Sharpsburg. Following his habit of caution, McClellan failed once more to commit his reserves. Just as Burnside's men seemed about to drive Lee's line back on itself late in the afternoon, they were hit hard on their left flank by A. P. Hill's Division. Hill had hurried his men up from Harpers Ferry, arriving just in time to stop Burnside's advance. By about five o'clock, the bloodletting had mercifully ground to a halt.

Henry Davenport was among the more fortunate that day. Though wounded, he survived the battle. He went on to participate in the Battle of Fredericksburg, was wounded twice at Chancellorsville and, on May 5, 1864, twice again in the Battle of the Wilderness.

Some of the day's heaviest fighting took place just south of Mumma's farm at the Sunken Road, known after the battle as Bloody Lane. Major General James Longstreet, Lee's senior corps commander, recalled that his men were "mowed down like grass before the scythe." Library of Congress.

Henry was hit yet again five days later at Spotsylvania and taken prisoner. He was held at Point Lookout, Maryland, until July 25, 1864, when he was transferred to Elmira, New York. He raised a few dollars by selling rings made from the buttons of his coat, and with his savings bribed a prison official to have his name placed on a list of prisoners to be paroled. Henry was exchanged on March 15, 1865, at Boulware's Wharf on the James River. He survived the war and settled in his hometown of Americus, where he married, raised a family, and lived a long and prosperous life as a farmer and merchant.

The joys of family, children, and fulfillment of life, so often taken for granted by most, were forever denied to a multitude of young men on that dismal Maryland battlefield. Among those so deprived was the young man from Marion County, Thomas Jefferson Rushin. After the battle, he was laid to rest in an unmarked grave.

The utter despair brought on by the loss of a loved one was felt time and time again in the days following Sharpsburg. More American soldiers were killed on September 17, 1862 than on any other single day before or since. Places with ominous names such as the Cornfield, Bloody Lane, the West Woods, Dunker Church, and Burnside's Bridge became memorials to nearly five thousand brothers, fathers, husbands, and sons who were forever taken from their families that day.[58] The carnage was such that, according to one account, "Antietam Creek . . . actually ran red."[59]

"A Smell of Death in the Air"

The coming of night hid the sight of a blood-soaked field from the eye, but the ear could not escape the screams and moans of thousands of wounded soldiers. One Confederate remembered the pitiful cries as being "much more horrible to listen to than the deadliest sounds of battle."[60] Men and boys lay scattered over the ground like human debris, injured in every imaginable fashion.

One of the more horrible forms of agony suffered at Sharpsburg involved the numerous haystacks that dotted the landscape. Throughout the day wounded men of both armies had crawled into the hay for shelter, but as the battle progressed many of these stacks were set afire by bursting shells. The helpless boys, bled too weak to move, were burned alive.[61]

From dusk to dawn soldiers combed the field looking for friends they had lost during the battle. According to one soldier, "half of Lee's army was hunting the other half."[62] But in the darkness, a disabled man was almost as likely to be trampled as assisted. Some horsemen, like Major Henry Kyd Douglas of Stonewall Jackson's staff, found it impossible to guide their animals through this sea of human misery and simply dismounted to make their way on foot.

Those fortunate enough to be found and removed from the field were in many cases only slightly better off, particularly by modern standards, than their hapless comrades. As inept as the medical profession was in dealing with then unknown causes of infection, medical conditions in both armies were made even worse by an indifferent attitude on the part of high-ranking government and military officials. The prevailing view among these august individuals was that "the business of war is to tear the body, not mend it."[63] Abraham Lincoln himself once referred to the Union's Sanitary Commission, a volunteer relief organization, as the "fifth wheel to the coach."[64]

This lack of concern was vividly reflected on the fields around Sharpsburg. Medical supplies on hand proved so inadequate that corn leaves had to be substituted for bandages.[65] One disgruntled surgeon complained, "I am tired of this inhuman incompetence, this neglect and folly, which leave me alone with all these soldiers on my hands,

On the evening of September 18th, Lee ordered a general retreat, and the army slipped back into Virginia taking what wounded it could. Thousands were left behind because there were not enough wagons to carry them all. Buel and Johnson, Battles and Leaders.

five hundred of whom will die before daybreak unless they have attention and I with no light but a five-inch candle."[66]

The next morning, as it became apparent that neither side would renew the conflict, unofficial truces were declared along most of the line so that the business of tending to wounded soldiers could begin in earnest. Local residents took in many of the less critical cases. The more seriously wounded were moved to nearby barns, which had been converted to field hospitals. Some soldiers were assisted by friends while others made their ways to the field hospitals under their own steam. One poor Southerner, with a leg shot off, hauled himself to the nearest aid by using two rifles as crutches.[67]

In describing one of the makeshift hospitals at Sharpsburg, a Southern correspondent wrote, "There is a smell of death in the air, and the laboring surgeons are literally covered from head to foot with the blood of the sufferers."[68] Another witness recalled that the doctors, in their blood-soaked apparel, looked like "a bevy of butchers."[69] No doubt the doctors themselves felt somewhat akin to butchers. With limited time and a seemingly unlimited supply of suffering men, the amputating saw found much use. The frequency with which surgeons employed the saw created what one man referred to as "puddles of human gore."[70] Another agonized youth recalled that "While sitting awaiting the surgeon, every few minutes an attendant would bring past me, to the open window, an arm, a leg, or a mangled hand, which he pitched into a little trench dug under the window."[71] This particular young man was more fortunate. His upper arm wound was not serious enough to warrant amputation, but the process by which the surgeon reached this happy determination was itself nearly as painful. "The young surgeon thrust his finger into the hole where the bullet had entered, and with his other forefinger plunged into the place of its exit, he rummaged around for broken bones, splinters, etc., until I swooned away."[72]

On the evening of September 18, Lee ordered the army's retreat to Virginia. Preparations began shortly after sunset, and around midnight the Confederates slipped away. Many of the wounded had to be left behind since there were not enough ambulances to carry them all. However, some of those who were able to secure a ride did not fare much better. A young Johnny Reb of Brigadier General Maxcy Gregg's Brigade recalled the plight of one group of wounded in an abandoned ambulance wagon on the northern side of the Potomac.

> At the edge of the river, and in the water, stood an ambulance filled with wounded men. The cowardly driver had unhitched his horses, crossed the river, and had left his suffering comrades to the mercy of the foe. The poor fellows begged piteously to be carried to the other side. General Gregg lifted his hat, and said to his soldiers, "My men, it is a shame to leave these poor fellows here in the water! Can't you take them over the river?" In an instant a dozen or more strong men laid hold on the ambulance and pulled it through the water, in most places waist deep, amid the shouts of the rest, who sang, "Carry me back to old Virginia."[73]

Then there was the plight of the walking wounded. Thousands of them crowded the roads between Sharpsburg and the Potomac, but the army could ill afford to be slowed down by these unfortunates. Were McClellan's men to catch it north of the Potomac, the Army of Northern Virginia, along with the government it defended, would in all likelihood cease to exist. Those who could not keep pace with the army were left by the roadside to be picked up by the Yankees.[74]

Daybreak on the nineteenth found the Confederates back in

A lone Johnny Reb left on the battlefield at Sharpsburg. This photo was taken on the Mumma farm two days after Lee's retreat.

Confederate dead gathered for burial on the Mumma Farm. The body of Thomas Jefferson Rushin may have been among them. Library of Congress.

Virginia. Cautions as ever, McClellan failed to follow up his victory with an aggressive pursuit, allowing Lee's army the time it needed to slip away. Disgusted with McClellan's continued timidity, Lincoln fired him within weeks. Still, the battle gave Lincoln the opportunity he needed to unveil the Emancipation Proclamation. In making freedom for the slaves an official Union objective, the proclamation changed the entire nature and course of the war.

Although the fighting wore on for another two and a half years, its single most bloody day was over. But in a very real sense, for those who lost friends and loved ones during that awful September, it was never really over. If lessons could be learned from such experiences, certainly among the most valuable for the common soldier dealt with a less romantic aspect of war. If they did not already know it, the boys of both North and South gained the certain wisdom that, in the words of one Johnny Reb, "the glory of war was at home among the ladies and not upon the field of blood and carnage . . . where our comrades were mutilated and torn by shot and shell."[75]

NOTES

1. E. Porter Alexander, *Military Memoirs of a Confederate* (New York: Charles Scribner's Sons, 1907), 223.

2. Bell I. Wiley, *Johnny Reb* (Baton Rouge: Louisiana State University Press, 1978), 120.

3. John H. Worsham, *One of Jackson's Foot Cavalry* (New York: Neale Publishing, 1912), 14.

4. George S. Bernard, ed, *War Talks of Confederate Veterans* (Petersburg, Va.: Fenn and Owen Publishers, 1892), 20.

5. Ibid.

6. Douglas Southall Freeman, *Robert E. Lee*, 4 vols. (New York: Charles Scribner's Sons, 1935), 2: 339.

7. Heros von Borcke, *Memoirs of the Confederate War for Independence*, 2 vols. (New York: Peter Smith 1938), 1: 234.

8. Helen Dortch Longstreet, *In the Path of Lee's Old War Horse* (Atlanta: Caldwell Publishing, 1917), 22.

9. Stephen Sears, *Landscape Turned Red: The Battle of Antietam* (New York: Tichnor and Fields, 1983), 83.

10. *Southern Historical Society Papers*, 52 vols. (Richmond: Southern Historical Society, 1876-1959), 10: 511.

11. Herman Hattaway and Archer Jones, *How the North Won* (Chicago: University of Illinois Press, 1983), 244.

12. *Harper's Weekly*, September 27, 1862.

13. *Southern Historical Society Papers*, 10: 511.

14. George M. Neese, *Three Years in the Confederate Horse Artillery* (New York: Neale Publishing, 1911), 112.

15. Draughton S. Haynes, *The Field Diary of a Confederate Soldier* (Darien, Ga.: Ashantilly Press, 1963), 20.

16. W. W. Blackford, *War Years With Jeb Stuart* (New York: Charles Scribner's Sons, 1945), 146.

17. Haynes, *Field Diary*, 13.

18. Richard Wheeler, ed., *Voices of the Civil War* (New York: Thomas Y. Crowell Company, 1976), 181.

19. Clifton Johnson, *Battlefield Adventures: The Stories of Dwellers on the Scenes of Conflict* (Boston: Houghton Mifflin, 1915), 119.

20. Clarence C. Buel and Robert U. Johnson, eds., *Battles and Leaders of the Civil War*, 4 vols. (New York: Century, 1887-88), 2: 687.

21. John Dooley, *John Dooley: Confederate Soldier—His War Journal*, edited by Joseph T. Durkin (Washington, D. C.: Georgetown University Press, 1945), 26.

22. G. Moxley Sorrell, *Recollections of a Confederate Staff Officer*, edited by Bell I. Wiley (Jackson, Tenn.: McCowat-Mercer Press, 1958), 103.

23. Ibid.

24. W. M. Owen, *In Camp and Battle with the Washington Artillery of New Orleans* (Boston: Tichnor, 1885), 130.

25. James V. Murfin, *The Gleam of Bayonets: The Battle of Antietam and the Maryland Campaign of 1862* (Baton Rouge: Louisiana State University Press, 1965), 107.

26. Borcke, *Memoirs*, 1: 236.

27. Ibid., 237.

28. A. L. Long, *Memoirs of Robert E. Lee* (Secaucus, N.J.: Blue and Grey Press, 1983), 222.

29. *O.R.*, series 1, vol. 19, part 2, p. 606.

30. Alexander, *Memoirs*, 223.

31. Bernard, *War Talks*, 21.

32. Dooley, *War Journal*, 25.

33. Bernard, *War Talks*, 21-22.

34. Hopkins, *From Bull Run to Appomattox*, 52.

35. Susan Williams Benson, ed., *Berry Benson's Civil War Book* (Athens: University of Georgia Press, 1962), 27.

36. Douglas Southall Freeman, *Lee's Lieutenants*, 3 vols. (New York: Charles Scribner's Sons, 1944), 2: 149.

37. Sorrell, *Recollections*, 101-02.

38. *O.R.*, series 1, vol. 19, part 2, p. 622.

39. James Dinkins, *Personal Recollections and Experiences in the Confederate Army* (Cincinnati: Robert Clarke Company, 1897), 53.

40. Buel and Johnson, *Battles and Leaders*, 2: 621.

41. Long, *Memoirs of Robert E. Lee*, 208.

42. Borcke, *Memoirs*, 208.

43. Dooley, *War Journal*, 27.

44. Ibid., 30.

45. Henry Kyd Douglas, *I Rode With Stonewall* (Chapel Hill: University of North Carolina Press, 1940), 152.

46. Wheeler, *Voices of the Civil War*, 183.

47. H. B. McClellan, *I Rode With Jeb Stuart* (Bloomington: Indiana University Press, 1958), 125.

48. Henry Steele Commager, ed., *The Blue and the Gray: The Story of the Civil War as Told by Participants*, 2 vols. (New York: Bobbs-Merill Co., 1950), 1: 215.

49. J. Cutler Andrews, *The South Reports the Civil War* (Princeton, N. J.: Princeton University Press, 1970), 216.

50. Sears, *Landscape Turned Red*, 85.

51. Shelby Foote, *The Civil War*, 3 vols. (New York: Random House, 1974), 1: 702.

52. Information on Thomas Jefferson Rushin is drawn from the United States Census Bureau, Seventh Census of the United States, 1850; Thomas Jefferson Rushin, Compiled Service Records, National Archives, Washington, D.C.; Rushin Papers, Georgia Department of Archives and History, Atlanta; William A. Frassanito, *Antietam: The Photographic Legacy of America's Bloodiest Day* (New York: Charles Scribner's Sons, 1978), 99-104; Lillian Henderson, comp., *Roster of the Confederate Soldiers of Georgia*, 6 vols. (Hapeville, Ga.: Longina and Porter, 1959-64), 2: 244; Nettie Powell, *History of Marion County, Georgia* (Columbus, Ga.: Historical Publishing, 1931), 165; Henry W. Thomas, *History of the Doles-Cook Brigade* (Atlanta, Ga.: Franklin Publishing, 1903), 334.

53. Information on Henry Thomas Davenport is drawn from Thomas, *History of the Doles-Cook Brigade*, 246; U.S. Census, 1850; Henry Thomas Davenport, Compiled Service Records, National Archives, Washington, D.C.; Henderson, *Roster of the Confederate soldiers of Georgia*, 2: 165; *Americus City Directory, 1891-93* (Americus, Ga.: The Americus Times Publishing Co., 1893), 28; William Williford, *Americus Through the Years* (Atlanta, Ga.: Cherokee Publishing, 1975), 65; Davenport Papers, University of Georgia, Athens.

54. Lee's official report puts the strength of his army at "less than 40,000 men" (*O.R.*, series 1, vol. 19, part 1, p. 151). Thomas Livermore gives the Federals just more than 87,000 present for duty. See Thomas L. Livermore, *Numbers and Losses in the Civil War* (Bloomington: Indiana University Press, 1957), 92.

55. This account of the 12th Georgia Regiment's participation in the battle is based on accounts from Thomas, *History of the Doles-Cook Brigade*, 222-24; Shepard Green Pryor Letters, University of Georgia, Athens; *O.R.*, series 1, vol. 19, part. 1, p. 976.

56. Bruce C. Catton, *The Army of the Potomac*, 3 vols. (Garden City, N.Y.: Doubleday, 1962), 1: 259.

57. Thomas, *Doles-Cook Brigade*, 223.

58. According to the figures of Thomas Livermore, 4,808 men and boys were killed at Antietam on September 17, 1862. Livermore, *Numbers and Losses*, 92-93.

59. Stewart Brooks, *Civil War Medicine* (Springfield, Ill.: Charles C. Thomas, Publisher, 1966), 39.

60. Douglas, *I Rode With Stonewall*, 174.

61. Buel and Johnson, *Battles and Leaders*, 2: 161-62.

62. Douglas, *I Rode With Stonewall*, 174.

63. Brooks, *Civil War Medicine*, 9.

64. Ibid.

65. Ibid., 86.

66. Ibid., 9.

67. Catherine S. Crary, ed., *Dear Belle: Letters From a Cadet and Officer to His Sweetheart, 1858-65* (Middleton, Conn.: Wesleyan University Press, 1965), 156.

68. Andrews, *The South Reports the Civil War*, 212.

69. Wheeler, *Voices of the Civil War*, 90.

70. Andrews, *The South Reports the Civil War*, 212.

71. Wheeler, *Voices of the Civil War*, 90.

72. Ibid., 91.

73. McClellan, *I Rode With Jeb Stuart*, 133.

74. H. H. Cunningham, *Doctors in Gray* (Baton Rouge: Louisiana State University Press, 1958), 129.

75. Watkins, *Co. Aytch*, 21.

HOMEFRONT: THE ORDEAL OF GEORGIA

"A Rich Man's War"

Soon after the Battle of Sharpsburg, Lee wrote to President Jefferson Davis, explaining that his army's strength was "greatly decreased by desertion and straggling. This was the main cause of its retiring from Maryland."[1] Desertion had been a problem from near the war's beginning and it continued to worsen as the war dragged on. Why did so many Johnny Rebs abandon the army? There were many answers to that question, the harsh realities of army life not least among them. But some hint of a broader discontent could be found in a Georgia newspaper editorial written in April 1865, only days before the Civil War ended.

> This has been "a rich man's war and a poor man's fight." It is true there are a few wealthy men in the army, but nine tenths of them hold positions, always get out of the way when they think a fight is coming on, and treat the privates like dogs. . . . There seems to be no chance to get this class to carry muskets.[2]

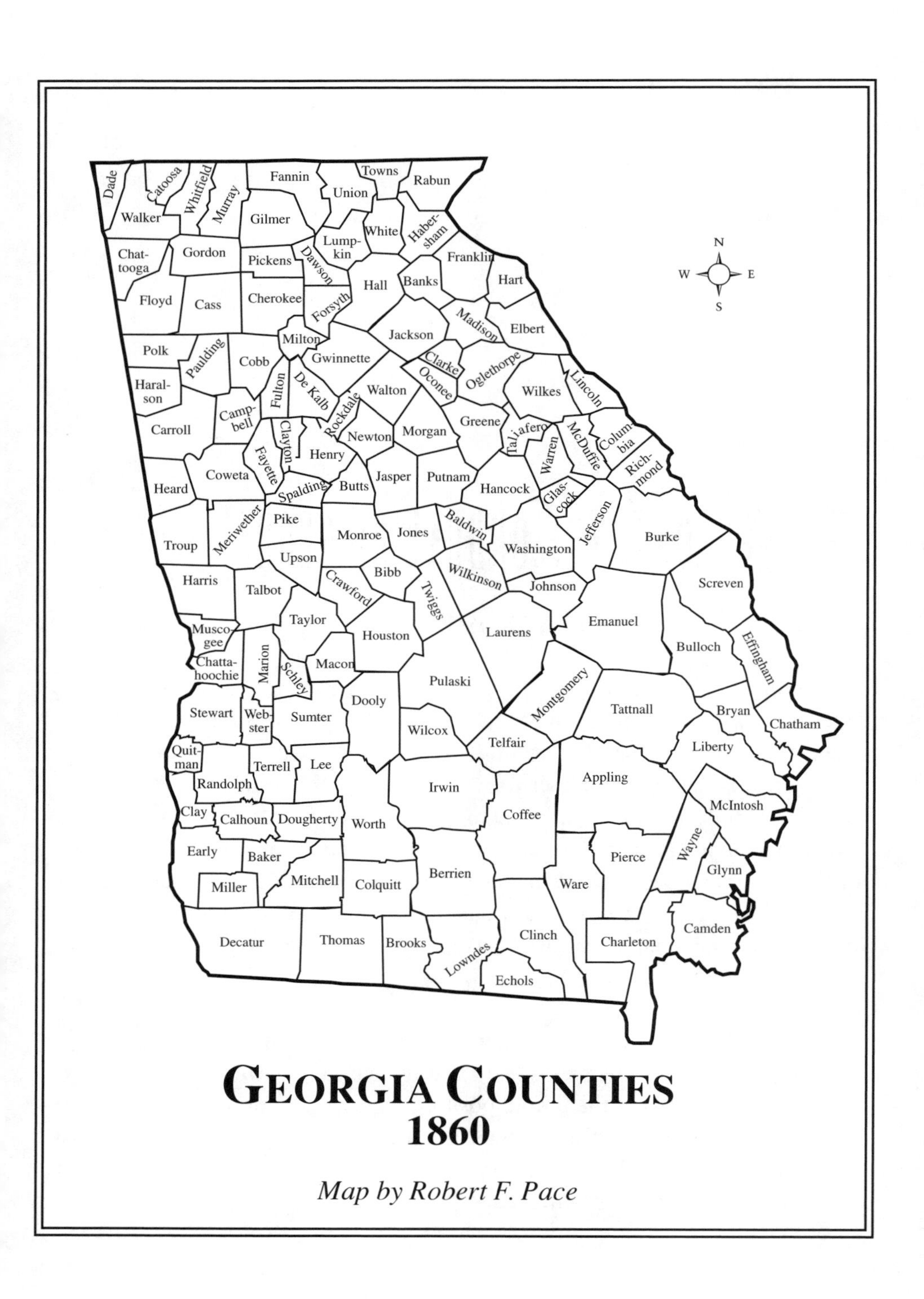

GEORGIA COUNTIES 1860

Map by Robert F. Pace

Such sentiment was by no means isolated. Throughout the Confederacy, soldiers and civilians alike expressed an increasingly hostile attitude toward the region's wealthy elite and even the Richmond government itself. Desertion and draft evasion became commonplace. By 1864 the draft law was nearly impossible to enforce and two thirds of the Confederate army was gone.

Even before the Confederacy came into being, signs that a Southern republic might have difficulty maintaining popular support, not to mention an effective fighting force, were clear. More than half the South's white population, most of whom owned no slaves, opposed immediate secession.[3] Nevertheless, state conventions across the South, all of them dominated by slaveholders, threw caution to the wind and took their states out of the Union. A staunch South Carolina secessionist frankly admitted that most Southerners were against it. "But whoever waited for the common people when a great move was to be made," he insisted. "We must make the move and force them to follow."[4]

Despite their general reluctance to secede, Southern whites showed considerable enthusiasm for the war after the firing on Fort Sumter and President Abraham Lincoln's call for an invasion of the South. But Southern enlistments, like those in the North, declined rapidly after the first major battle at Manassas. The Confederacy's response to its recruitment problem was an early indicator of the role class issues would play in the wartime South.

In April 1862 the Confederate Congress passed the first national conscription act in American history. Like the North's later draft, men of wealth could avoid military service by hiring a substitute or paying an exemption fee. And slaveholders who owned twenty or more slaves were automatically excused from the draft. This twenty-slave law was perhaps the most widely hated act ever imposed by the Confederacy, especially for poor soldiers already in the ranks. Said one Southern private, "It gave us the blues; we wanted twenty negroes. Negro property suddenly became very valuable, and there was raised the howl of 'rich man's war, poor man's fight.'" He continued, "From this time on till the end of the war, a soldier was simply a machine. We cursed the war . . . we cursed the Southern Confederacy. All our pride and valor had gone."[5] Not surprisingly, desertion became an even greater problem for the Confederacy than for the Union. By 1864, Jefferson Davis himself admitted that "two-thirds of our men are absent . . . most of them without leave."[6]

Another practice that helped turn thousands of Johnny Rebs against the Richmond government was the confiscation of private property, or "impressment." Soldiers resented the fact that their families back home were forced to give up a portion, sometimes a major portion, of their meager produce, while the more politically influential planters were left alone. That they had to sell at prices set by the government was even more galling. But it usually did not matter what the prices were. All farm families got in exchange were promissory notes, usually unredeemable, or inflated paper currency that was nearly as worthless. Very often they got nothing at all. One Georgia woman complained bitterly that "the country is plum full of [Confederate] cavalry just . . . stealing all the time."[7] John Hagan, a soldier from southwest Georgia, confirmed that assertion in a letter to his wife: "I believe our troops are doing as much harm in this country as the Yankees . . . and in fact where this army goes the people is ruined." He was certain that the Confederacy could never survive while handling its own people so roughly.[8]

Poor and middling farm families bore the brunt of impressment, mainly because they offered easier targets than did the planters. Smaller farmsteads tended to grow more food products anyway, which was what the impressment agents wanted. For the planters, old habits were hard to break. They continued to devote much of their acreage to cotton at a time when thousands of soldiers and civilians were starving. The result was an ever increasing desertion rate and food riots throughout the South.

The Confederate government could not survive without support from its own people, and that fact was widely acknowledged during the war. "If we are defeated," announced one Atlanta newspaper, "it will be by the people at home."[9] And so the Confederacy was defeated: by arrogant planters, greedy capitalists, corrupt officials, and most of all by disillusioned Johnny Rebs.

Perhaps nowhere could the divisive role of the Southern class system be viewed more clearly than in South's keystone state of Georgia. Primarily an agricultural region, its population ran the socioeconomic scale from planters and lesser slaveholders down through landed yeoman farmers to landless tenant farmers and slaves. In addition to the rural farming folk, there were merchants, factory workers, skilled artisans and craftsmen, urban professionals, and industrial entrepreneurs. Most studies of Confederate defeat have focused on military strategy and tactics. But an examination of what went on behind the lines and the impact it had on soldiers' attitudes may reveal even more about why the Civil War ended as it did.

"Give Me the Sword"

By 1860 Georgia was among the Cotton Kingdom's most prosperous states. Such prosperity, however, was by no means shared by all residents. Most lived in conditions that were regarded even at the time as abject poverty. Of Georgia's one million residents, nearly half were slaves. The great majority of the state's white inhabitants engaged directly in agriculture, but only half owned three or more acres of land. Many of the rest were tenant farmers, sharecroppers, or day laborers, all working land owned by someone else. A majority of landholders also owned slaves, but two-thirds held fewer than ten. Most of these small slaveholders worked the fields along with their slaves and had a lifestyle not so different from that of many non-slaveholding yeomen. Only the planters (men who owned twenty slaves or more) and their families benefited significantly from an economic system based primarily on landholding, cotton and slavery. This group made up just three percent of the population.[10]

What the small farmers wanted, of course, was to become big farmers. That had been possible in the 1820s and 1830s, when land was cheap following the expulsion of the native Creek and Cherokee peoples. By the 1850s, however, land and slaves were so expensive that few small farmers had any real hope of ever moving into the planter class. Yet it was these plain folk who had to be convinced of their stake in the preservation of slavery and an independent Southern nation for the

Confederacy to survive. It would ultimately prove an impossible task.

Signs of Southern disunity were apparent long before the war began. In Georgia, thousands of residents argued against secession even after Lincoln's election. Led by men like Alexander Stephens and Benjamin Hill, unionists held rallies throughout the state, urging caution among their fellow citizens. In Stewart County, "a large number of citizens" attended an anti-secession meeting led by P.H. Gregory, L. Bryan, and James L. Wimberly. They nominated three of the county's most prominent citizens, John C. Byrd, Simon Holt, and Charles H. Warren, to represent their views in the upcoming campaign for delegates to Georgia's secession convention.[11]

Union sentiment was so strong in neighboring Randolph County that secession men feared that the tide was turning against them. In a letter to Howell Cobb, one of the state's leading secessionists, they asked, "Where are all our speakers? We have done what little we can here but there is great need for missionaries [of secession] in every part of the State." They urged Cobb to take a short tour through southwest Georgia to bolster the waning enthusiasm for secession.[12]

On November 20, 1860, less than two weeks after Lincoln's victory at the polls, Governor Joseph E. Brown signed a bill that called for the election of delegates to Georgia's secession convention. Balloting took place on January 2, 1861, and the convention met two weeks later at Milledgeville, the state capital. The popular vote was close, with a slight majority of 42,744 to 41,717 opposing immediate secession.[13]

When the secession convention met at the state capital of Milledgeville, Eugenius A. Nisbit proposed a test resolution for secession to gauge the feeling of the delegates. Enough of the delegates who had been elected on a promise to vote against secession were enticed by the promise of a slaveholder republic to pass the resolution by a vote of 166 to 130. The next day, with more delegates switching sides, the convention approved an ordinance of secession 208 to 89.[14] It could hardly have been surprising that the convention ultimately favored secession in spite the popular vote. While only a third of Georgia's electorate owned slaves, 86 percent of the convention delegates were slaveholders.[15]

In speaking for the secessionist cause just after Lincoln's election, Robert Toombs, who owned a plantation in Stewart County and was one of the state's most prominent secessionists, expressed his determination to see Georgia out of the Union regardless of the popular will. "Give me the sword!" he demanded of his fellow Georgians. "But if you do not place it in my hands, before *God I will take it*!"[16] Responding to Toombs' threat, an anti-secessionist editor in west Georgia's Upson County wrote, "Let him take it, and, by way of doing his country a great service, let him run about six inches of it into his left breast."[17] But Toombs and his powerful secessionist allies were so well organized that by the time the state convention met it was too late to stop them.

The remaining unionist convention delegates urged that the secession ordinance be put to a vote of the people. Fearing the outcome of such a move, secessionists refused. Georgia, like the other seceding states, left the Union without submitting the issue to a direct popular vote.[18] In February, Georgia representatives, along with others from the Deep South, met in Montgomery, Alabama, to form the Confederate States of America. Two months later, on April 12, 1861, Confederate artillery opened fire on Fort Sumter in Charleston Harbor, setting off the bloodiest conflict in American history.

"The Legal Right to Withdraw His Name"

In the wake of Sumter, so many men rushed to military service that the Confederacy could not arm them all. Thousands of volunteers had to provide their own weapons or secure the backing of wealthy patrons. Like most Georgia units, the Miller County Wild Cats were left to arm themselves "with every death-dealing instrument that could be procured." Typically, each man carried a Bowie knife along with an old rifle or shotgun. One elderly man, who had tried without success to talk his son out of going to war, finally gave in and presented him with what was surely a prized possession—a single-barrel shotgun. "I don't want any war," the old man told his boy, "but if you will go, here's old Betsy; take her and give the Yankees hell."[19]

Several factors accounted for the widespread surge of volunteering, fear of Yankee invasion foremost among them. There was also regional identity, desire for upward mobility, peer pressure, and even a sense of adventure.[20] Whatever their misgivings about the planters and slavery itself, thousands of yeomen and poor whites took up arms in the spring and summer of 1861. Georgia alone had furnished over eighteen thousand volunteers for Confederate service by May 4, second only to Virginia.[21] It came as little wonder that the state's rail system was in chaos. According to one source, lines were clogged with trainloads of raw recruits, "whose enthusiasm for the Confederate cause was equaled only by their lack of any clear conception as to the authority under which they were to serve, or of their destination."[22]

It seemed that almost everyone was caught up in the excitement of what they thought surely would be a short conflict. Assuming, as they did, that one Southern boy could whip ten Yankees, how could it be otherwise? Even men who could not join the army offered to serve in other areas. Thomas Coleman of Cuthbert, a physically impaired bookkeeper, wrote to Governor Brown, asking for "a situation in some place to enable me to help support the government."[23]

Despite the mass volunteering and general excitement, there were early signs that support for the war, and for the Confederacy itself, might not last long. Many Georgians continued openly to support the Union. In counties such as Sumter, Greene, Troup and Lumpkin, it was dangerous to express Confederate sympathies.[24] When vigilantes led by Harrison W. Riley threatened to seize the U.S. mint in Dahlonega and hold it for the Union, Governor Brown sent no troops to stop them. He knew sentiment in the region was with Harrison and his gang.[25] Officials in Pickens County flew the U.S. flag over the courthouse for weeks after secession.[26] Private citizens did the same. Randolph L. Mott of Columbus, a longtime Union man, kept the Stars and Stripes flying from the cupola of his home. Some considered the home the only place in Georgia that had never been out of the Union.[27]

Expressing popular sentiment in Walker and Dade counties, James Aiken wrote to Governor Brown in February 1861, insisting that he and his neighbors would never submit to the secession con-

Georgia Governor Joseph E. Brown. University of Georgia Libraries.

vention's decision. It had taken Georgia out of the Union not for the good of its citizens, but for "those that owns lands and Negroes!" He begged the governor to allow Georgia voters to decide the issue directly, promising to abide by the outcome. But if Brown refused, there were 2,500 volunteers prepared to defend northwest Georgia's right to secede from the state and rejoin the Union. "If we cannot get it one way," he warned, "we know how we can get it at the point of the bayonet and the muzzle of the musket. We are just as willing as you ever seen mountain boys."[28]

People across the South expressed doubts about the legitimacy of secession. In Georgia, Governor Brown did not announce the results of the January 2 vote for convention delegates until late April, and that was only at the insistence of concerned voters. Even then he lied about the figures. Brown insisted that the secessionists had won by more than 13,000 votes, when in fact they were almost certainly defeated by a margin of some one thousand.[29]

With the Confederacy now an established fact, many Southerners were more concerned about how the war might affect the South in general, and themselves in particular, if it did not end quickly. The consequences of an extended conflict were evident enough to those on the front lines. When soldiers of the 15th Alabama Regiment, many of whom were from southwest Georgia, arrived in Virginia and visited Manassas a month after the battle, they found hundreds of shallow graves scattered over the fields. Rain had washed much of the dirt away and skeletal remains protruded from the ground. Hogs were feeding on the dead.[30] It was not what the young men had expected to find. Few had allowed themselves to imagine what the horrors of war were really like in the immediate post-Sumter excitement. But after Manassas, the soldiers had no choice. It was of little surprise that so many, especially those from non-slaveholding families, began to reexamine their motives for volunteering. In late July, just ten days after Manassas, Joel Crawford of Quitman County wrote to Governor Brown, wanting to know "if after the signing of a written instrument binding the signer to go to the present war, if any signer thereof has the legal right to withdraw his name."[31]

"A Set of Ignoramuses"

Besides the horrors of the battlefield, there was a growing awareness among the men in the ranks that their personal sacrifices were likely to be much greater than those of the Southern elites. This class disparity became clear early on, when the Confederate government, lacking weapons enough for all its volunteers, allowed those who could provide their own to enlist for only one year instead of three. That meant purchasing the expensive .577 caliber Enfield rifles, which few common soldiers could afford. Most volunteers were not

Georgia soldier John C. Curtright wrote home on October 6, 1862, trying to calm his wife's fears: "Knowing the uneasiness you constantly feel about me, nothing I can write will keep you from feeling so, but . . . from past protections & safteys we can with confidence ask for a continuation of these." Two days later he was killed at the Battle of Perryville and buried a few miles away near Harrodsburg, Kentucky. Years after the war the grave was discovered by a nephew who had Curtright moved home to LaGrange where today he lies buried next to his wife in the Hillview Cemetery. Johnson, Campfire and Battlefield.

informed until they reached the front lines that their shotguns and squirrel rifles would not do for military service. Many poor soldiers found that their one-year enlistments had suddenly turned into three. As one historian put it, "the price of being a patriot was higher for the common man than for the rich man, three times higher to be exact."[32]

As the war entered its second year, the gap between rich and poor widened. While the planters sacrificed luxuries and suffered some inconveniences, soldiers' families and other plain folk faced a daily struggle just to stay alive. This situation was hardly a formula for unity among Southern whites. When a "village belle" in Blakely, Georgia, said she "could get along without stockings so long as she had fashionable dresses," the editor of the *Early County News*, E.H. Grouby, labeled her and others like her "a set of ignoramuses."[33] As Grouby clearly recognized, most planters had little understanding of the plight of common folk.

One of the most severe hardships to confront families back home was excessive inflation. At First, few thought it would be a problem, since the war was expected to end quickly. Even after First Manassas, some scoffed at the blockade and its economic threat. Others, however, were more farsighted. John B. Lamar, Howell Cobb's brother-in-law, wrote to the politician-general in November of 1861, "we can laugh at the blockade for a while if salt is $12 a sack," but he wondered what the impact would be if the blockade lasted another year. "It makes me hold my breath when I think of it."[34] Less than a year later the blockade grew even tighter, and salt was selling $125 a sack when it was available at all. It had been only two dollars before the war.[35]

Such dramatic price increases for even the most basic commodities were not uncommon. Butter went from twelve cents a pound in 1861 to seventy-five cents two years later. By the end of the war it was five dollars or more. Corn that was two dollars a bushel in 1863 sold for fourteen by February 1865. Bacon went from twelve cents to fifty cents a pound in the war's first year. By the end of the war a pound of bacon was four dollars. Flour that sold for nine dollars a barrel before the war was going for four hundred by war's end. Coffee went to thirty dollars a pound shortly after the war began and from there to sixty and seventy dollars. The cost of more potent beverages was on the rise as well. Rum that was purchased for just seventeen cents a gallon in Cuba sold for twenty-five dollars after being run through the blockade. That was an increase of nearly 15,000 percent.[36]

Although the blockade contributed to rising prices, even more damaging to the economy was profiteering and speculation by planters and merchants. In his study of Columbus, Georgia, during the Civil War, Diffee Standard concluded that the blockade was an excuse rather than the reason for inflated prices.[37] As early as November 1861, one Georgia man complained to Confederate Vice President Alexander Stephens that "common farmers" were finding it difficult "to keep our heads above the flood of destruction" brought on by "the money thieves, those Speculators."[38] With food supplies dependent as they were on small farmers, if those farmers were forced under by wild speculation the Confederacy might go with them. E.H. Grouby saw the danger as well. Those who engaged in profiteering (Grouby called them "home Yankees") were "by far greater enemies to the South and do more to injure her cause than ten times their number of Yankees in the field." Such people, said Grouby, "carry their patriotism in the *pocketbook*."[39]

As if private speculation was not bad enough, government contractors and high-ranking military officers were also guilty of profiteering. Duncan Jordan of the firm Lennard and Jordan, a small shoe manufacturing company in Cuthbert, complained to Governor Brown in November 1861 about the practices of government purchasing agents. He had been selling his shoes to the government at low prices, thinking they were going to the army. He later discovered that the agents were selling his shoes on the open market at inflated prices. Jordan suggested that the state make "application through honest agents" and void contracts with "avaricious Speculators."[40]

Less than a year later, scandal rocked the War Department when quartermaster officers were discovered embezzling funds from sales to speculators of food supplies bound for frontline soldiers. Congress responded by making it illegal for the public to buy military supplies from enlisted men but said nothing of officers. But the act hardly put a dent in the problem of corruption. It served only to emphasize the South's pervasive class divisions. The *Early County News* denounced the legislation for its blatantly elitist overtones.

> Why is it not also against the law to buy any of these articles from Quarter Masters, Commissaries, &c., when it is a well known fact that many of these swoll head gentry steal a great deal of this kind of Government property which they have in their possession, to be distributed among the needy Soldiers, sell them, and pocket the money? There is more rascality, according to the number, among officers than privates. Why are not officers bound up as tight as privates? There is altogether too much *favoritism* shown to little jackass officers by Congress.[41]

Another exasperated Georgia citizen added his voice to the swelling chorus urging Governor Brown to take decisive action. "Do for God's sake put an end to this unrighteous war. We shall be eaten up by Confederate Office holders and Speculators."[42]

The flood of pleas from anguished citizens and the impact of inflation and speculation on the currency could not long be ignored.

In December 1861, Governor Brown signed legislation that outlawed speculation in all sorts of basic commodities, including "clothing, shoes, leather, cloth of any kind, provisions, wheat, flour, corn, cornmeal, meat, bacon, hogs, cattle, salt, bagging, rope, and twine." Penalties for violation ranged from $500 to $5,000.[43] Confederate officials also tried to address the inflation problem by appointing price commissioners in every state and congressional district. It was the commissioners' job to fix prices on items deemed common and necessary. Even local citizens tried price fixing in an effort to ease their plight. A public meeting headed by M.T. Alexander and W.W. Fleming, held in Early County, attempted to regulate prices of homegrown produce.[44] Despite all efforts to curb it, profiteering continued. Joe Brown was sure that speculators and profiteers were the Confederacy's greatest threat, but admitted that the anti-speculation laws in Georgia were a "dead letter."[45]

"Sooner Than All Lincolndom"

Speculators posed an obvious threat to the Southern economy, but, as Brown seemed to recognize, they became an even greater threat to the war effort. Volunteering dropped by the winter of 1861-62, and new recruits hardly could be expected to come from the ranks of the plain folk. Already they felt that they were being starved by those who benefited most from the war.

Even so basic a thing as food became a mark of social distinction. Of course, the wealthy had eaten much better than the poor even before the war. But now malnutrition and starvation threatened thousands of soldiers and their families while planters fed themselves as well as ever. To make matters worse, planters continued to grow cotton even as the plain folk and the army faced starvation. Though the Confederate government had imposed a ban on cotton exports in an attempt to force recognition and intervention by Britain and France, planters continued to stockpile cotton for future sale. Many ignored the embargo and smuggled cotton out of the South. Most did not expect the war to last very long. But even if it went on for years, it could not last forever. When it was finally over, planters hoped to make millions by selling their precious fiber to cotton-hungry textile mills in the North and in Europe. With their vision firmly fixed on the promise of future wealth, southern planters failed to heed the warning signs that their shortsightedness was undermining the Confederate cause.

One indignant Georgian from Albany wrote to Governor Brown, outlining the problem of cotton overproduction in his region and imploring the governor to do something about it.

> We are in great danger of *Subjugation* to the hated government that we are resisting, *not* by the army of demons invading our country, but by *avarice* and the *menial Subjects* of King cotton. . . . I hear of one planter who is pitching 900 acres in cotton, the overseer of another told me he is going to plant 300 acres, another . . . 90 acres, another 300 acres, and two others full crops of cotton. And so it will be all over the state. . . . The country needs all the grain that can be raised, the producing forces, both in men and horses are greatly diminished, while the demand for grain is increased. I hope your Excellency will adopt some plan to stop those internal enemies of the country, for they will whip us sooner than all Lincolndom combined could do it.[46]

Joe Brown was already well aware of the problem. He knew perhaps better than any political leader in the South that support for the Confederacy among the plain folk and even among the soldiers was fragile. Many already saw planters as the source of their economic woes. If the people were forced to go hungry while wealthy land owners planted cotton, Brown worried about what the consequences might be. During the first year of the war, in an "Appeal to the People of Georgia," he urged the planters to grow less cotton and more food.[47] But all his urging fell on deaf ears. By 1862, Georgia planters were growing so much cotton that the warehouses could not hold it all.

When it became clear that the Confederate government would take no direct action against planters, Joe Brown tried to

TO PLANTERS.

OUR Warehouse being full, Planters will please stop consignments of Cotton to our care until further notice.

DILLARD, POWELL & CO.

Columbus, Ga., Sept. 3, 1862. 2m.

Adding to the burdens of soldiers in the field and of their families back home, planters grew so much cotton that the warehouses could not hold it all. The result was a food shortage so severe that it literally helped starve the Confederacy out of existence. One Georgian wrote to Governor Brown, begging him to bring planters under control, "for they will whip sooner than all Lincolndom combined could do it." Columbus Enquirer, *September 16, 1862.*

regulate cotton production on his own. In November 1862 he asked the General Assembly to impose a tax on "each quantity of seed cotton sufficient to make a bale of four hundred pounds . . . produced next year . . . over what is actually necessary for a home supply." The Assembly rejected Brown's suggestion of a tax on seed cotton. After all, many of the legislators were planters and were not eager to place a tax on themselves. But they did make it illegal for anyone to plant more than three acres in cotton for each slave owned or farm hand employed. Any landowner who violated this law would be fined $500 for each acre of cotton beyond the three-acre-per-hand limit.[48]

Such legislation, however, inspired little fear among planters. According to one source, "not one acre in fifty in the best corn district in Georgia was planted in corn."[49] A frustrated Governor Brown responded by asking Georgia's legislature to restrict the cotton crop to only one-fourth an acre per hand and "make it highly penal" for anyone to exceed that limit. The Assembly refused and, despite continued urging from Brown, ignored the issue for the rest of the war.[50]

In direct violation of state law and Confederate policy, "planters insisted," as one man put it, "on their right to grow unlimited amounts of cotton; to retain it for sale whenever they chose; and to sell it whenever, and to whomever, they chose."[51] And it did not seem to matter who the buyers were. Planters and cotton merchants would sell to anyone, even the Yankees. According to one estimate, more than half a million bales of Southern cotton were smuggled to the North between 1861 and 1865.[52] Two men from Fort Gaines reported to Governor Brown in March 1862 that cotton smuggling was common-

Planters continually ignored the government's ban on cotton exports. Cotton growers in southwest Georgia regularly smuggled their produce down river to the gulf port of Apalachicola on boats like the Shamrock, *built in Columbus during the war, where it was transferred to oceangoing vessels. Some planters bragged openly that the longer the war went on, the more money they made. Florida State Archives.*

place in southwest Georgia. Steamboats typically made their way up the Chattahoochee River, loading cotton bales as they went, with Columbus their supposed destination. But somehow, much of the cotton seemed to find its way to the Gulf port of Apalachicola, Florida. There it was transferred to vessels that took "pleasure excursions" out to see the blockading Union fleet, always returning with empty cargo holds. The Fort Gaines men described cotton smuggling as such a fact of economic life for southwest Georgia planters that no intelligent man in the region could doubt it.[53]

Why would the South's planters and merchants provide cotton to clothe Union armies while those of the Confederacy went lacking? The simple fact was that the North paid better and the planters knew it. Some openly bragged that the longer the war went on, the more money they made.[54]

"If He Were a Poor Man He Would Be Hanged"

With such a lucrative black market in cotton, it was little wonder that planters were not anxious to concentrate on growing food. But scarcity forced food prices up and speculation drove them even higher. Rampant inflation inevitably followed, making planters and smaller farmers even less willing to exchange what food they had for increasingly worthless Confederate currency.

By 1863, in what became a turning point for attitudes toward the war and the Confederacy, the Richmond government determined that what it could not buy it would take by force. That summer the Confederate Congress passed a series of taxes on everything from occupations to incomes. The most significant was a 10 percent confiscation levy on such farm items as livestock, wheat, corn, oats, rye, hay, fodder, buckwheat, sweet potatoes, Irish potatoes, sugar, cotton, wool, tobacco, peas, beans, and peanuts. Even this tax-in-kind did not provide enough food to meet military needs. So the government began to confiscate these items, and anything else it wanted, far beyond the 10 percent level.

Though no member of any class held impressment in high regard, yeomen were concerned that the wealthy did not contribute their fair share. As always, impressment agents first sought out the most vulnerable targets—the farmsteads of soldiers' families and other plain folk. Only when these farms were stripped bare did they turn to the plantations. Even then, planters were reluctant to part with their surplus. Some used political connections to avoid impressment. Others simply hid their supplies.

A Georgia soldier recalled how planters "would hide their wagons under straw piles, and carry off their horses where you cannot come at them. . . . Some of these men [are] rich—worth fifty thousand dollars."[55] One Georgia planter stashed at least a thousand bushels of corn in a large crib hidden deep in the woods near his plantation. "What kind of a man can he be?" asked the local newspaper editor. "Is he a friend of the country? No; for no man who is will, at such a time as this, hide his corn from suffering Soldiers and their families." The editor insisted that he ought to be lynched. "He is a meaner man, by far, than any Yankee that ever invaded our country."[56]

The reluctance of planters to make sacrifices led increasing numbers of soldiers and their families to conclude that the raging conflict was a rich man's war.[57] When Robert Toombs used political connections to have himself exempted from impressment, one Georgia newspaper lashed out. "We believe Toombs, because he is rich, does pretty much what he wants . . . if he were a poor man he would be hanged." The editor concluded that "a *poor* man in this world has no more showing than a blind dog in a meat house with a dozen starving Yankees after him."[58]

Georgia's Assembly recognized the dangers of general destitution and took some few steps to alleviate it. Its efforts, however, were plagued by confusion and corruption.

In May 1862, the state relief agent in Miller County wrote to Governor Brown asking for clarification on how he should distribute the salt ration. "The salt which by your order was sent to Miller County has come to hand," the agent wrote, "and there is great need of it." But, he continued, there was "some difference of opinion" over who should receive it. Was it for the families of all soldiers then in service or only for those in service when the order was issued? And did the order include both Confederate and state troops, or only one group? If only one, which one?[59]

The next year Miller County's acting Justice of the Peace, George W. Cleveland, wrote Brown accusing the local relief agent of "swindling." Noting that "none of our soldiers families has drawn any money since the first of August and the agent reports no money on hand," Cleveland asked Brown what the county's appropriation was supposed to be. The state legislature had allocated $2.5 million for aid to soldier's families statewide, but none was getting to the many indigent families of Miller County. Cleveland emphasized the urgency of his request: "Some of our brave soldiers families are in very destitute conditions and must soon suffer if not relieved in some way."[60]

Even local soldiers' aid societies, so active at the war's outset, had almost disappeared. "What has become of the Soldiers' Aid Society of Early County?" asked editor E.H. Grouby in March of 1864. "We haven't heard anything of it lately. We hope our noble ladies have not concluded to cease their efforts to assist our brave Soldiers."[61] This admonishment spurred the society to renewed action, but its efforts were half-hearted at best. A few months later Grouby published a list of the meager contributions received by the Soldiers' Aid Society. "It is with *shame* for our citizens that we publish it," he wrote, "for there are many, *very many*, in our county who are well able to give *bountifully* who have not contributed a cent, while those who have, have given a very small mite." Grouby advised the Soldiers' Aid Society to "hang up the fiddle and the bow, for the people are too infernal hard-hearted and selfish to give a poor Soldier a mouthful to eat."[62]

"What Will Become of the Women and Children"

On top of all their other difficulties, the most severe hardship suffered by soldier's families was the absence of their men. Letters from soldiers to their wives were filled with regret at not being home and advice on what to do until their return. In November 1863, William Asbell wrote to his wife Sarah from Camp Cobb in Decatur County: "I have received both of your letters and was glad to hear Through Them that you are all alive but sorry to know that the children are sick on your hands when I cannot be there to assist you with Them." Asbell told Sarah to feed their hogs corn once a day and potatoes the rest of the time. "If the children are not able to dig the potatoes," he said, "fence of a portion of the patch for [the hogs]." As the weather grew colder and food ran low, William wrote his wife, "You had better try and sell one or other of the horses . . . as you are scarce of Provisions. You will have to do the best you can."[63]

For many women laboring under the burdens of inflation, impressment, sick children, and absent husbands, their best was simply not good enough. Thousands of petitions from women all across the South describing their desperate situation and begging for relief flooded into Richmond. Typical of these was the following, dated September 8, 1863, from the women of Miller County.

> Our crops is limited and so short . . . cannot reach the first day of March next . . . our fencing is unanimously almost decayed . . . . But little [illegible] of any sort to rescue us and our children from a unanimous starvation. . . . We can seldom find [bacon] for none has got but those that are exempt from service by office holding and old age and they have no humane feeling nor patriotic principles. . . . An all wise God who is slow to anger and full of grace and mercy and without respect of persons and full of love and charity

By the war's second year the food shortage was taking a heavy toll on soldiers' families. They lived on what little they could grow or beg from men of privilege. One Georgia resident noted that poor women were "sometimes offered assistance at the sacrifice of their honor, and that by men who occupy high places in church and State." Harper's Weekly.

> that he will send down his fury and judgement in a very great manner [on] all those our leading men and those that are in power if there is no more favors shown to the mothers and wives and of those who in poverty has with patriotism stood the fence Battles . . . . I tell you that without some great and speedy alerting in the conducting of affairs in this our little nation God will frown on it and that speedily.[64]

The women received no favors from the Davis administration. Worse yet, military officials denied their husbands the opportunity to help. Family starvation was not generally considered a valid reason for granting furloughs. It would have done Miller County's women little good in any case. Just a day after they signed their petition, the Miller County Wildcats were captured at Cumberland Gap, Tennessee, and spent the rest of the war in an Illinois prison camp.[65]

Abandoned and starving, thousands of women became beggars just to keep their families alive. Leaving children at home for days or weeks at a time, they roamed the countryside pleading for food. Sympathetic railroad conductors and steamboat captains occasionally provided transportation, but most often the women made their way on foot. Some planters gave what they could to the women; others did not. But even the more generous viewed these unfortunates with contempt. One planter called the starving women "perfect nuisances."[66]

While soldiers and their families faced the threat of starvation, wealthy Southerners enjoyed a lifestyle hardly touched by the war. As late as March 1865, only weeks before the war's end, Kate Cumming wrote of a meal at the Cook House in Columbus during which the table was so heavy with food the it "actually groaned." Frank Leslie's Illustrated Newspaper.

Impressment, taxation, inflation, starvation, and no help from callous government officials or planters—it was all too much for many women. Hundreds took matters into their own hands and turned to stealing rather than see their children starve. After all, so much had been taken from them, they saw themselves as taking back only what was theirs in the first place. Many women took food from plantations whether the planters offered it or not. Women in Miller County were known to steal livestock on a regular basis. At one point, a group of about fifty soldier's wives raided the government depot in Colquitt and took a hundred bushels of corn. In a letter to the *Macon Telegraph*, a sympathetic local resident blamed Miller County's inferior court judges for the women's plight. "These gentlemen are more busily engaged in their own business than they are in attending to their judicial duties. In fact, they don't seem to bestow any time at all toward relieving the necessities of suffering families of soldiers, as they are in duty bound by law to do." John Davis, a well-to-do slaveholder and judge of the inferior court, disagreed. Destitution had nothing to do with such raids, he insisted. It was simply in the nature of these women to steal.[67]

Attitudes like this were common among the upper classes. As early as 1862, Godfrey Barnsley, a wealthy Bartow County planter, complained that "the character of the population here . . . is growing worse." "Thieving," he said, "in no small way" was among their character flaws.[68] Few openly acknowledged the obvious link between desperate circumstances and desperate acts. But ignoring the problems of

Hunger became so widespread that food riots broke out in cities throughout the South including Richmond, Virginia. A mob of about sixty-five women in Columbus, Georgia, some armed with pistols and knives, marched down Broad Street, looting stores as they went. Similar riots occurred in Atlanta, Macon, Augusta and Savannah. Smaller towns like Stockton, Marietta, Thomasville, Cartersville, and Blackshear saw riots as well. In Valdosta, a crowd of starving women broke into a government warehouse and made off with a wagonload of bacon. Fifty Colquitt women attacked the local depot and stole 100 sacks of corn. Frank Leslie's Illustrated Newspaper.

hunger and speculation only made them worse. By 1863, food riots were breaking out in major cities all across the South, including the Confederate capital of Richmond. In Georgia, a band of women attacked a wagon near Thomasville and made off with three sacks of corn. Another group broke into the government warehouse in Valdosta and stole a wagonload of bacon. When an Atlanta merchant told one of his customers that bacon was $1.10 a pound, she drew a pistol and took what she needed, prompting other women in the store to do the same. From there, they moved on to nearby stores, paying whatever prices they wanted or nothing at all. Similar riots broke out in Macon, Augusta, Marietta, Forsyth, Cartersville, Hartwell, and Blackshear. A crowd of starving women numbering perhaps a hundred rioted in Savannah, looting several stores on

Whitaker Street. And on April 10, 1863, a mob of about sixty-five Columbus women, some armed with pistols and knives, marched down Broad Street "to raid the stores of speculators."[69]

A few days later, Daniel Snell of Harris County wrote home to his wife Sarah, "You spoke of a riot in Columbus . . . it is no more than I expected. I understand there was also one in Augusta . . . . What will become of the women and children with the food situation?"[70] Indeed, thousands of soldiers wondered how their families would get along in their absence. With government corruption out of control and the planters unwilling to help, many began to question whether the Confederacy was worth preserving at all, much less fighting for. As the war lumbered on and conditions worsened, more and more soldiers decided it was not.

"Honey, Why Don't You Come Home"

The worsening condition of their families was clear enough to the soldiers. Letters from home described the struggles of destitute wives, often pleading for their husbands to come home. Mary Brooks was left with three young children, a baby not yet weaned, and a farm to run near Greenville. She wrote to her husband Rhodam, "I never get any rest night or day, and I don't think I will last much longer." She was running low on bacon and salt as well as money with which to purchase them. "It is money for everything," she said, "so you may know it is getting low with me."[71]

Most soldiers had little or no money to send home. "The private's pay," recalled one Southern infantryman, "was eleven dollars per month, if he got it; the general's pay was three hundred dollars per month, and he always got his."[72] Enlisted men went without pay for months at a time. One Georgia soldier wrote home about how the officers in his regiment received their pay while the men in the ranks got none. In response, the enlisted men laid down their arms until the payroll arrived. "The [colonel] and others of our officers said that we were rebelling against our country," he wrote, "but we deny the charge it was not so. We were only rebelling against those haughty officers, for not giving us our rights—and other tyrannizing over us."[73]

Money was only a secondary concern for soldiers' wives. What they really wanted was for their husbands to come home. Mary Jane Curry of Decatur County wrote to her husband, "I had such a pleasant dream last night. I though you was at home and expected to remain."[74] Sallie Lovett spoke in moving terms of how the days dragged by as she waited for her husband Billie's return.[75]

> Troup County, March 26, 1862
>
> My dearest husband:
>
> It is with a sad and heavy heart I take my pen in hand to write you a few lines. I received your very welcome letter last evening, glad indeed to hear from you and hear you was getting along so well. For it is more than I am. Billie, I am in so much trouble this evening. I have looked for you so hard today. I thought you would be sure to come. . . . Every time I hear a train I go to the door. I say, well, I do hope Billie [will] come down on that train. I wait and look until dinner. Then I say, well, I do hope he will come this evening. I wait until dark. No Billie yet. Then I bring a long sigh, perhaps a tear and say, well, I don't know why he don't come. Every time I hear a noise towards the gate I run to the door, but what do I see: nothing but trees and bushes. I strain my eyes almost out of their sockets but no Billie can I see. I turn 'round with a sigh. To think he has forgotten me! . . . I am not living any now, only breathing. It is true I am well in body but not at heart. My heart is grieved, the worst of all diseases. Honey, why don't you come home?

Like so many other Southern women, Sallie cared much more for her family than anything else. "I would give a world of Confederacies," she told her Billie, "just to be with you."[76]

The soldiers, of course, wanted to come home just as much as their wives wanted them to. But it was difficult for an enlisted man to get a furlough. William Asbell wrote from his station in Decatur County that none of the men were getting furloughs and there was "no telling" when any would be granted. A month later, furloughs were still unavailable.[77]

If furloughs were hard to get, discharges were nearly impossible to come by. One Georgia private said of his commander, "This damned general won't give you a furlough or a discharge till you are dead ten days, and *then* you have to prove it."[78] William Andrews, a sergeant from southwest Georgia, recalled a soldier who found that the only way to get out of the army was to shoot his left hand off. "That," wrote Andrews, "ended his soldiering."[79]

Failing to get permission from the army for their men to come home, thousands of women turned to Governor Brown for help. Susan Thurman of Lumpkin asked Brown to declare her husband exempt from service. All his brothers and brothers-in-law had been killed in the army and he was needed at home to help their widows and children.[80] A Decatur County woman, Mrs. Aliff Williams, wrote to Brown on behalf of her brother. He was home on sick leave suffering with bronchitis and chronic asthma and was unable to return to duty. "Besides," she wrote, "he is a poor man with a wife and a hand full of little children [and] a widowed mother."[81]

Brown received another letter from a poor woman in Stewart County who had lost her husband, two brothers-in-law, and a brother to the war. She had one brother left, and he was in the army sick with typhoid fever, measles, and a "hacking cough." She begged the governor to discharge her brother so he could recover and care for his three children. "Their Mother is dead," she wrote, "and his Mother is a widow and not able to do anything for them."[82] Despite such heartbreaking pleas few enlisted men who could walk and carry a rifle were allowed to leave the army.

One thing that alienated poor soldiers almost as much as the government's inability to care for their families (and its refusal to allow them to do so) was the ease with which wealthy soldiers got furloughs and discharges. The higher one's rank or the greater one's wealth, the easier it was. As one Johnny Reb put it, "A general could resign. That was honorable. A private could not resign . . . and if he deserted, it was death."[83] The right to act according to the dictates of one's conscience was a privilege that the South's self-styled aristocracy reserved for itself.

Thousands of Southern men faced the dilemma of whether to allow their families to die at home or risk death themselves by deserting. And the risk was very real indeed. Despite the danger, however, soldiers deserted by the thousands. Presenting their rifles as furloughs to anyone who dared challenge them, they made their ways over hundreds of rugged miles to help their starving families. Some never made it. Many of those who did were dragged back to the army in chains. William Andrews wrote that it was "an everyday occurrence for men to get letters from home stating that their families are on the point of starvation. Many a poor soldier has deserted and gone home in answer to that appeal, to be brought back and shot for desertion."[84]

The way the soldiers saw it, they had very little choice. If the government could not care for their families, the soldiers had to. Their first duty was to the survival of their wives and children. Even those with no families starving at home had great sympathy for those who did. William Andrews, a bachelor, insisted that he too, faced with the same situation, would desert. "Thank God," he wrote, "I have no wife and children to suffer on account of an ungrateful government."[85]

"This Tyrannical Conscription Law"

Family hardships, hunger, cold, disease, and class antagonism brought on by special privileges for the rich and highly placed—all these contributed to a general decline of enthusiasm for the war. So weak was support for the Confederacy by the spring of 1862 that officials in Richmond feared the war might soon be lost. The army badly needed men, but few would willingly come forward. Willing or not, though, as far as the government was concerned they had to come.

In April of 1862 the Confederate Congress passed an Enrollment Act that gave the president authority to force young men into the military with or without their consent. Under the terms of this act, commonly known as conscription or the draft, white males between the

Confederate Vice President Alexander H. Stephens declared slavery the "cornerstone" of the Confederacy, which only reinforced the "rich man's war" attitude among common folk. He should have known they would. A fellow planter had only recently written to Stephens, expressing his belief that if the issue were left to poor whites, slavery would soon be ended. Stephens himself feared the ultimate consequences of disunion and spoke against it as a delegate to Georgia's secession convention. Even after his appointment to the vice presidency, Stephen's commitment to the Confederacy was questionable He was constantly at odds with Jefferson Davis, accusing him of taking on unwarranted dictatorial powers. He left Richmond in 1863 and joined Joe Brown in calling for peace. He was among the earliest opponents of the draft, calling it "radically wrong in principle and in policy." Cleveland, Alexander H. Stephens.

ages of eighteen and thirty-five became subject to involuntary military service. As an inducement to enlist before the draft went into effect, the government offered a cash bonus to those who volunteered and allowed them to serve with units of their choice. Fearing they would be drafted anyway, hundreds of reluctant men volunteered in March and early April of 1862. One was John Joseph Kirkland of Early County. A small farmer who owned no slaves, Kirkland had a wife and five children when he enlisted with the Early Volunteers. He was thirty-three, only two years short of exemption. A year later he lost a leg at the Battle of Chancellorsville.[86]

To plain folk, the most offensive provisions of the draft act were those allowing wealthy men to avoid service. Those with enough money could hire a substitute or simply pay the government an exemption fee.

Fearing they would be drafted in any case, some men joined the army just before the draft went into effect so they could get the fifty-dollar enlistment bonus and serve with units of their choice. John Joseph Kirkland of Early County, a slaveless small farmer and the author's great-great-grandfather, had a wife and five children when he enlisted as first corporal with the Early Volunteers in March 1862, a few weeks before the draft began. He was 33, only two years short of exemption. His younger brother Jacob joined the Early Volunteers as well and two months later was killed in Virginia. John Joseph had the heartbreaking duty of escorting the body home to their mother. A year after that, having fought through the Peninsula Campaign, Second Manassas, Sharpsburg, and Fredericksburg, he was nearly killed himself when a bullet shattered his right leg at the Battle of Chancellorsville. The leg was amputated just below the knee. After the war he moved to neighboring Miller County and served for some years as county treasurer and tax collector. He was also a trustee of Union Missionary Baptist Church. He died in 1904 at age seventy-five and was laid to rest in the church cemetery beside his wife Amanda Bush Kirkland. Courtesy of Martha Bush Kirkland, Miller County, Georgia.

Few but the most affluent could do either of these. And then there was the infamous twenty-slave law, which excused planters from the draft outright. Though few seemed to realize it at the time, this one law defined the nature of the war for an entire class of Southerners. From 1862 until the conflict's end, for the great mass of Southerners, it was a rich man's war. Confirmation of that fact was especially evident in the newspapers. One Georgia paper ran an ad reading "WIFE WANTED—by a young man of good habits, plenty of money, good looking and legally exempt from Confederate Service."[87]

Governor Brown, claiming state rights, opposed the Confederate draft, but levied one himself for the state militia.

Notice to Absentees.

IN accordance with an order from Maj. G[illegible] McLaws, all Absentees of Early Volunteers, Co. "A.," 51st Ga. Vol's., who are absent on sick furlough, and which have expired, are ordered to report immediately to their command, or furnish a certificate from an Army Surgeon, or they will be dealt with as deserters.

SANFORD ALEXANDER,
Capt. Com'd'g Co. A., 51st Ga. Vol's.
June 24, 1863. 36-tf

To Soldiers.

ALL Soldiers now, or who may be absent from their Commands, excepting those who are disabled by wounds from reporting at Macon, are hereby ordered to report to their Commands immediately at the expiration of their furloughs, or they will be subject to arrest, by order of Lieut. Col. Harris. I trust all Soldiers will respect this order, and save me the unpleasant task of sending them to Head-Quarters.

J. H. SAUNDERS,
Sub. En. Officer of Early Co.
Nov. 4, 1863. 4-2m paid

The year 1863 was not a good one for the Early Volunteers or any of the county's other military companies. So many Early County men were absent without leave that warnings were posted in the Early County News *encouraging them to return. They were testimony to a rising tide of disaffection with the Confederacy.*

Planters avoided Brown's draft by bribing state enrolling officers or using their influence in local courts to have themselves declared exempt. Judge Richard Henry Clark of Georgia's southwestern judicial district granted exemptions to planters on a regular basis, and Colonel Carey Styles, commanding southeast Georgia's fifth military district, offered exemptions for $1,000 to anyone who could afford to pay.[88] One way or another, men of means who desired to do so had little difficulty evading military service. It seemed increasingly obvious that this was a rich man's war, which made the problem of desertion even worse.

When one Georgia farmer was drafted, he complained bitterly to a neighbor: "They've got me in this war at last. I didn't want to have any thing to do with it any how. I didn't vote for Secession—but them

Wealthy men could avoid being hauled off by a conscript company by paying an exemption fee, hiring a substitute, or bribing the local conscript officer. Plain folk who could afford none of these options had little choice. Library of Congress.

are the ones who have to go & fight now—and those who were so fast for war, stay out."[89] Plain folk expressed similar attitudes throughout the state. "The people of Georgia regard the draft as disgraceful," Captain George A. Mercer insisted.[90] Another Georgia soldier, Edward R. Harden, wrote from Camp Jackson, "The army here is in great excitement. . . . I find everybody opposed to this tyrannical conscription law."[91] William Andrews, along with five other men of the 1st Georgia Regiment, hung a conscript officer in effigy as a way to "make our intentions known to them." They erected a gallows, stuffed a uniform with Spanish moss, and hung the thing up with a sign around its neck reading CONSCRIPT OFFICER. "It was never found out who done it," Andrews wrote, "and that was the last thing heard of a conscript officer coming to our camps."[92]

Conscript officers were among the most detested men in the South. According to one account, conscript patrols went "sweeping through the country with little deference either to the law or the regulations designed to temper its unavoidable rigor."[93] A Johnny Reb from Georgia wrote that conscript officers were everywhere, "watching for some poor devil who is trying to keep out of the army." He told of soldiers running men down with hounds and dragging them off to the army in chains. One Georgia draft dodger was caught disguised as a woman. The man was chained and delivered to his company wearing the dress in which he was captured.[94]

There seemed to be no limits to which conscript officers would go in quest of recruits. Even a man's physical condition made little difference to them. Men in the poorest of health were sometimes dragged from their homes and forced into service. Those with enough ready cash, however, could usually persuade conscript officers to pass them by. One Georgia editor wrote, "It is strange to us that the Government allows its officers to conscript poor men who have the appearance of *dead men*, while they turn loose rich ones who are *young, hale and hearty*."[95]

Resentment toward conscription was evident throughout Georgia. A report from Franklin County made it clear that there were so many deserters and draft dodgers in the county that conscription efforts were useless.[96] One conscript officer was nearly killed when he tried to enforce the draft law at Fort Gaines. Threats to his life became so serious that he fled the state.[97] Resistance to the draft was rampant all across the South. Howell Cobb thought it would take the whole Confederate army to enforce conscription. The law, he said, threatened the Confederacy "as fatally as . . . the armies of the United States."[98]

But conscription was an established fact and thousands of letters poured into both state and Confederate offices requesting exemption from the draft. Potential draftees cited any number of reasons why they should be excused. Isaac Bush of Colquitt asked for exemption on account of "my ankles swelling." For B.J. Smith of Cuthbert, leaving home would mean leaving his "large warehouse" with three thousand bales of cotton unattended.[99] Those who could not get exemptions outright tried to avoid military service by other means. When the Confederacy made county officials exempt from the draft, such positions became the focus of heated campaigns. In Early County thirty-seven candidates vied for five seats on the Inferior Court. "But there was no politics in the race," said one county resident. "The candidate just wanted the office to keep him out of the war."[100] M. W. Johnson of Oglethorpe County, a soldier of the 6th Georgia Regiment, went home on furlough and had himself elected justice of the peace to keep from going back to the front.[101]

Residents of Carroll County formed a local guard unit to keep their men at home. Its members did little more than meet at the courthouse in Carrollton once every few weeks for muster. Local deserters were urged to join the guard as a way of keeping out of the Confederate army. One contemporary reported that "persons wishing to get their friends home from the army write them that they can come home and by joining this command, remain at home."[102] Some local guard units did not even bother with the farce of an occasional muster. Another unit near Dahlonega, composed entirely of draft dodgers and deserters led by a Colonel Findley, probably never met at all. When a Confederate officer was sent to investigate, he found the command "scattered over the country as if quartered at home." He felt it would be nearly impossible to round up these men and force them into the regular army.[103]

Such phony units were not unusual. Soldiers deserted at an ever increasing rate soon after conscription went into effect, and they usually enjoyed the sympathy of their friends and neighbors—which encouraged even more men to desert. Newspapers throughout Georgia were filled with long lists of deserter's names in the summer of 1862, some offering rewards for their capture and return. Thirty dollars was put up for the return of Fulton County native Thomas Miller. Similar rewards were offered for the return of E.J. Lewis of Hancock County, J.L. Morris of Wilkinson County, and John Burns of Augusta.[104] In July, the following notice appeared in the Augusta paper.[105]

> **DESERTED**
>
> $30 REWARD offered for the apprehension of each of the following. Wm. A Daniel, age 20, Co. A, Banks County Guards. Jere Martin, age 20, Co. D; A. S. King, age 24, Co. F; F. P. Williams, age 20, Co. F; John Huchins, age 26, Co. F. All from the 2nd Regiment of Georgia Volunteers. Reward will be paid on delivery to the jail at Augusta.

Such lists soon took up so much space that editors refused to publish them.

By October 1862, more than half the soldiers from northeast

Georgia alone had "skedaddled" and were hiding out in the mountains.[106] At least a third of Lumpkin County's "Blue Ridge Rifles" deserted. Nearly half the county's "Boyd Guards" did the same.[107] One Confederate officer reported to Secretary of War James Seddon that "the conditions in the mountain districts of North Carolina, Georgia, and Alabama menaces the existence of the Confederacy as fatally as either of the armies of the United States."[108]

"Our Freedom is Now Gone"

The increasing reluctance of Southerners to serve in the Confederate army reflected a much broader discontent. From its beginnings, many poor whites saw the conflict as a rich man's war. That view became more widely held among plain folk as the months dragged by. Planters brought the Confederacy into existence but would not grow corn enough to feed its soldiers or their families. Speculators were driving prices of even the most basic necessities far beyond the reach of most Southerners. The burdens of taxation and impressment fell heaviest on the small farmers, and it was they and the landless whites who bore the brunt of conscription. That disparity produced a class-based political consciousness among plain folk that made itself felt in the 1863 elections. Southern voters ousted nearly half their congressional representatives that year. Georgia voters sent nine new legislators to Congress, eight of them elected on platforms that opposed the Davis administration. Julian Hartridge of southeast Georgia's First District was the only member of the state's House delegation to retain his seat.[109]

Plain folk were active in local elections as well. In Columbus they offered their own slate of candidates for city office on the "Mechanics' and Working Men's Ticket." According to the *Columbus Enquirer*, the new party "prevailed by a very large majority" in the October 7 balloting. Its success sent shock waves through the ranks of the city's political establishment. Some went so far as to suggest excluding common folk from future elections by reinstituting extensive property qualifications for voting and office holding.[110]

The *Enquirer*'s editor gave voice to elitist fears just two days after the vote when he chastised plain folk for their "antagonistic" attitude and condemned the "causeless divisions of our citizens into classes."[111] Reaction to the *Enquirer*'s criticism was swift and direct. On October 13, a competing city paper, the *Columbus Sun*, ran a letter it received from a local man signing himself "Mechanic."

> **Voting by Classes**
>
> *Editor Daily Sun*:—I notice in the Enquirer, of Friday evining, an article complaining bitterly of the people voting by classes . . . He says, "there is certainly no ground for any antagonism in the city." In this the Enquirer is mistaken; for any man, woman or child can see that the people are dividing into two classes, just as fast as the pressure of the times can force them on. As for example: class No. 1, in their thirst for gain, in their worship of Mammon, and in their mighty efforts to appropriate every dollar on earth to their own account, have lost sight of every principle of humanity, patriotism, and virtue itself, and seem to have forgotten that the very treasures they are now heaping up are the price of blood, and unless this mania ceases, will be the price of liberty itself; for we know something of the feeling which now exits in the army, as well as in our work-shops at home. The men know well enough that their helpless families are not cared for, as they were promised at the beginning of the war. . . . They know, too, that every day they remain from home, reduces them more and more in circumstances, and that by the close of the war a large majority of the soldiery will be unable to live; in fact, many of them are ruined now, as many of their homes and other effects are passing into the hands of speculators and extortioners, for subsistence to their families. Thus you see, that all the capital, both in money and property, in the South, is passing into the hands of class No. 1, while class No. 2 are traveling down, soon to take their station among the descendants of Ham. You can easily see who are class No. 2. The soldiery, the mechanics,

> and the workingmen, not only of Columbus, but of all the Confederate States. In view of these things, is it not time that our class should awake to a sense of their danger, and in the mildest possible manner begin the work of self-defense . . . Then we claim the right, as the first alternative, to try and avert the great calamity, by electing such men to the councils of the nation as we think will best represent our interests. If this should fail, we must then try more potent remedies.

Efforts to find "more potent remedies" had already given rise to a loosely organized movement, widely known as the Peace Society, to end the conflict with or without Southern independence. The Peace Society was one of perhaps half a dozen secret or semi-secret organizations that sprang up across the South to oppose the war. Little is known of the Society's early days. It probably formed in north Alabama or east Tennessee during the spring of 1862 and later spread to Georgia. Though it was composed mostly of those who wanted nothing more than an end to the fighting, unionists were at the heart of the organization and remained its principal advocates throughout the war.

From the very outset of the Civil War unionism was surprisingly strong in the South. More than 100,000 white Southerners served in Union armies during the war, not counting those in irregular units who numbered many more.[112] Unionism found its greatest strength among whites in areas with few slaves such as the mountains of north Georgia and the pine barrens of the southeast. But even in black belt regions, where slaves made up more than half the population there were significant numbers of anti-Confederates.

In March 1862, John O'Connor of Fort Gaines warned Governor Brown of "spies and traitors" operating all along the lower Chattahoochee River.[113] General Howell Cobb was so concerned about anti-Confederate sentiment in southwest Georgia that he began to censor the postal service later that year.[114] E.H. Grouby noted in the *Early County News* that there were deserters "in every direction." One officer called the wiregrass "one of the greatest dens for Tories and deserters from our army in the world."[115]

Hunger, the draft, and a "rich man's war" attitude led thousands to oppose the war. So prevalent was antiwar feeling in northern Georgia the region became a stronghold of the Peace Society. It held secret meetings at which members swore allegiance to the Union and actively worked to spread antiwar feeling among soldiers and civilians alike. Harper's Weekly.

The situation was no better to the east. A Lowndes County resident warned Governor Brown of local deserters and draft dodgers throughout the piney woods of south Georgia. In October 1863 a Savannah man wrote that troops in southeast Georgia were demanding peace and would soon turn to mutiny or desertion if they did not get it. There were already considerably more than a thousand deserters hiding in the Okefenokee Swamp alone.[116] A few months later, an insurrection plot was discovered among troops at the Rose Dew Island batteries south of Savannah. Encouraged by local citizens connected with the Peace Society, the soldiers took an oath never to fight the Yankees, to desert at the earliest opportunity and encourage others to do the same.[117]

Antiwar sentiment in Georgia was so strong by 1863 that state and Confederate officials could do little against it. Popular support and innumerable hiding places made it nearly impossible to track down deserters and draft dodgers. The Bureau of Conscription's superintendent admitted that public opinion made it difficult to enforce the draft act. There was, he lamented, no disgrace attached to desertion or draft evasion.[118] One band of deserters quietly set up camp on an island in the Chattahoochee River. Family and friends kept them supplied with food and other necessities until the war was over.[119] Some deserters were more outspokenly defiant. In Stewart County, several men of the 3rd Georgia Regiment openly declared that they had no intention of returning to the army.[120]

Even when deserters and draft dodgers were captured, there was no guarantee of punishment. When a conscript company in Franklin County captured several deserters, the local jailor would not lodge them.[121] So strong was antiwar feeling that judges refused to hold court on draft evaders without a military escort. Even when trials were held, convictions were rare. Juries consistently refused to return guilty verdicts against those who opposed the war. General Howell Cobb conceded in August 1863 that to drag antiwar men into court was "simply to provide for a farcical trial."[122]

Frustrated by anti-Confederate sentiment on local juries throughout the South, in February 1864 Congress authorized Jefferson Davis to suspend the writ of habeas corpus and impose martial law. Officials could now make arrests without warrants and imprison suspects without a trial. The act only made matters worse. One enraged citizen, who signed himself "A Georgian," reacted in an open letter to the *Early County News*: "When this war broke out our people thought they had something to fight for, but now they have nothing, but to keep the Yankees checked, so that our own Government may oppress them more."[123] The paper's editor, E.H. Grouby, was in full agreement. "Our freedom is now gone!" he declared. "May the devil get the whole of the old Congress!" Grouby insisted that if only he had the money he would immigrate to Cuba.[124]

Despite empathy from local residents and their own growing numbers, life for deserters hiding out in the mountains and bottomlands was precarious at best. They were harassed by army patrols, and sympathizers had little food to give them. Some became so desperate that they fled to the Yankees. When Major General William T. Sherman's army entered north Georgia in the spring of 1864, hundreds of Confederate deserters greeted the invaders—so many that officials could not process them fast enough. Some were put to work as support troops for frontline Federal soldiers. They even helped the Yankees dig entrenchments in preparation for the assault on Rebel lines at Kennesaw Mountain.[125]

After Sherman captured Atlanta in September, hundreds of soldiers and civilians remained in the city and aided the Federal army.[126]

Later that year, during his famous March to the Sea, Sherman received at letter from Confederate deserters and draft dodgers from Liberty and Tattnall counties. In it they insisted that they opposed secession and offered Federal general their services in whatever capacity he saw fit.[127] Some went further than that. One gang of Georgia ex-Confederates led by Alonzo Rogers and Porter Southworth formed themselves into a battalion and called it the "Volunteer Force of the United States Army from Georgia."[128]

In Georgia's wiregrass region, deserters sometimes turned to the Union blockade fleet on the Gulf Coast for help. In early 1863 John Harvey, representing a group of 500 wiregrass deserters and draft dodgers, met with Lieutenant George Welch of the USS *Amanda* at Apalachicola, Florida, to discuss placing the men under protection of Federal authorities. Armed only with shotguns, they had been skirmishing with conscript companies for some time and their ammunition was running low. They preferred to be taken into protective custody either as prisoners or refugees but, according to Welch, added "that they would follow me or any other leader to any peril they are ordered to rather than leave their families and go north." Welch was sympathetic but declined, saying he did not have enough manpower to guarantee safe passage for that many men from that deep in enemy territory.[129] However, as Confederate strength along the Apalachicola declined, the Federals did begin to run ammunition and other supplies upriver to anti-Confederate partisans.

As their ranks grew through 1863, some of these groups of deserters formed guerrilla bands, described by one historian as "no longer committed to the Confederacy, not quite committed to the Union that supplied them arms and supplies, but fully committed to survival."[130] They raided plantations, attacked army supply depots, and drove off impressment and conscript officers. A Confederate loyalist in Fort Gaines begged Governor Brown to send a company of cavalry for protection against these raiders.[131] So did pro-Confederates in Dade and Walker Counties. A band of local deserters had threatened to burn the crops of any farmer in the region who expressed Confederate loyalties.[132]

Another deserter band known as Colquitt's Scouts terrorized res-

Deserters and draft dodgers were often belligerent. Some formed guerilla bands and attacked Confederate supply wagons, raided local plantations, and harassed impressment and conscript officials. Frank Leslie's Illustrated Newspaper.

idents of Floyd County until its leader, "Captain Jack" Colquitt, was finally killed.[133] In January 1863 Governor Brown sent the state militia to put down deserter gangs around Dahlonega with little success.[134] When authorities in Fannin County arrested members of one deserter gang in June 1863, some of their comrades, along with local sympathizers, mounted a violent rescue. Several "loyal citizens" were killed in the bloody gun battle. Only one deserter lost his life.[135] So brutal had Georgia's internal civil war become that the editor of Milledgeville's *Confederate Union* wrote, "We are fighting each other harder than we have ever fought the enemy."[136]

"Don't Think There is Much Regret for the Loss"

The rise of deserter bands was only the most violent reflection of widespread discontent with the Confederacy and the war. And, as the war entered its final year, few expected the Confederacy to survive for much longer. In a March 1864 *Early County News* editorial, E.H. Grouby wrote: "We cannot help thinking this is the last year of the war . . . we have now entirely too many little jackass upstarts filling positions in our government."[137] As Grouby's comment suggested, most Georgians were so disgruntled with the Confederacy by 1864 that they actually looked forward to its fall. In October of that year Grouby wrote that the only people who still backed the war effort were those who held "fat Government contracts" and corrupt officials who were "not yet done fleecing the Government. Their voice," he said, "is still for war, war, war!"[138]

Lacking any real political power, the voice of the common folk was expressed in local meetings throughout Georgia, where declarations were drawn up demanding an end to the war. The people of Wilcox County urged Governor Brown "to settle this Bloody conflict at once by negotiations before the whole white male populations is butchered up." A few such declarations were sent to General Sherman, insisting that the respective counties wished to rejoin the Union whether the state did or not. At one meeting in Thomas County, a fight broke out which the unionists won.[139]

An Early County resident expressed the class-conscious frustration of less affluent whites when he noted that there were planters who would not give a starving man a morsel of bread or meat, even if they knew it would save his life. His pen dripping with sarcasm, the writer asked, "Ain't it a pity but what the Yankees would take every thing such men have, and leave them without a single mouthful of anything? We hope to live to see the day."[140]

With Confederate defeat all but inevitable, the army's desertion rate continued to rise. Even those few who did not desert had little enthusiasm for the war. Most simply wanted to go home. Requests for discharges and extended furloughs flooded Confederate and state offices. From Randolph County came a petition to have Private B. F. Brooks relieved of duty. His wife Julia headed a list of twenty-six names pleading on his behalf.[141] Already at home on leave, Daniel Chessy of Steam Mill in Decatur County asked for an indefinite extension of his furlough.[142] West Sheffield of neighboring Miller County did the same.[143]

So many soldiers were leaving the ranks that the Confederacy's remaining supporters began seriously to consider what until then been unthinkable—freeing the slaves and arming them. As early as 1863, high-ranking Confederate officials had begun to advocate such a move. Already the North had almost 200,000 black men in uniform, three-fourths of them native Southerners. And they were proving to be very effective troops. As prospects for Confederate victory became ever more dim, support for arming slaves began to grow. By late 1864

Powerful Georgia politician and Confederate General Howell Cobb. University of Georgia Libraries.

Jefferson Davis and Robert E. Lee both favored the idea.

Not surprisingly, most slaveholders fiercely resisted any suggestion that slaves be placed in the military. They feared not only the loss of their "property" but also what slave conscription would mean for the future of the Confederacy and slavery itself. As early as March 1861, Vice President Alexander Stephens had said that the Confederacy was founded on what he called "the great truth" that blacks were not the equal of whites, and that slavery was their "natural and normal condition."[144] Howell Cobb summed up the prevailing racist view when he insisted that "the day you make soldiers of [slaves] is the beginning of the end of the revolution. If slaves will make good soldiers, our whole theory of slavery is wrong."[145]

Aside from its threat to the Confederacy's "great truth," there was the question of whether giving guns to blacks would make them supporters of the Confederacy. It was an unlikely assumption. To *Columbus Times* editor J.W. Warren, the idea seemed ridiculous. He was certain that slaves would never fight for the Confederacy even if they were freed. Warren's great fear was that they would join the Yankees as soon as they reached the front lines. If slaves were armed, he warned, "we will ourselves, take the best in the country, drill and train them, and then hand them over—ready made warriors—to the enemy."[146]

Warren was probably right. Throughout the war, Georgia blacks had resisted their enslavement in subtle and overt ways, sometimes finding whites willing to help them. Willis Bone, a white man, frequently hid both deserters and runaway slaves on his Irwin County farm. In spring 1862, Calhoun County authorities arrested three local whites for supplying area slaves with firearms in preparation for a rebellion. Two years later, slaves in Brooks County conspired with John Vickery, a white community resident, to stage an uprising.[147] And when William T. Sherman's Federal army went rampaging through Georgia in late 1864, thousands of blacks escaping bondage followed after them.

Despite slaveholder objections and the plan's unlikely success, on March 13, 1865, the Confederate Congress finally passed legislation that authorized the recruitment of up to three hundred thousand blacks. But here was no promise of freedom for those who agreed to serve.[148] It hardly mattered. By then it was too late.

The next month, in April 1865, the last major Confederate armies surrendered. On May 10 Yankee troopers captured Jefferson Davis near Irwinville, Georgia, as he fled south in a vain effort to get out of the country and establish a Confederate government-in-exile. Other Rebel officials were soon in custody and the Confederacy ceased to be.

In a sense, though, the Confederacy as a nation never really existed at all. Eminent Georgia historian E. Merton Coulter, enamored as he was with the Lost Cause, could still admit that the Confederacy never became an "emotional reality" to most of its people.[149] Even at its beginning the Southern Confederacy lacked firm support. Less than half of white Southerners favored secession in the first place. A

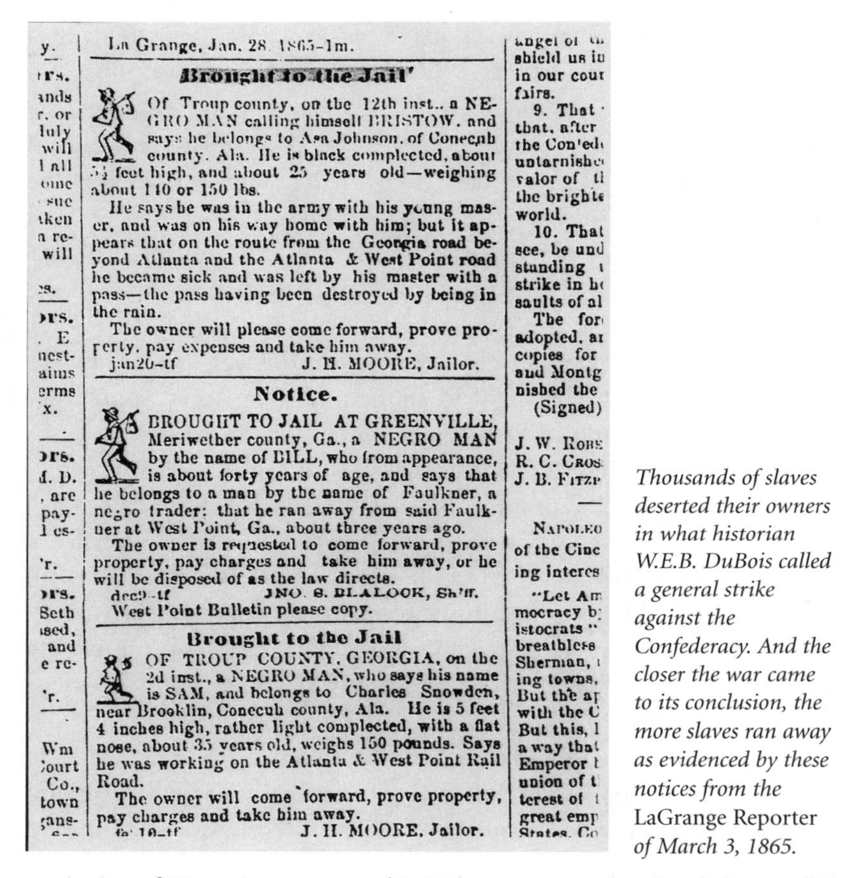

La Grange, Jan. 28, 1865–1m.

Brought to the Jail

Of Troup county, on the 12th inst., a NEGRO MAN calling himself BRISTOW, and says he belongs to Asa Johnson, of Conecuh county, Ala. He is black complected, about 5½ feet high, and about 25 years old—weighing about 140 or 150 lbs.

He says he was in the army with his young master, and was on his way home with him; but it appears that on the route from the Georgia road beyond Atlanta and the Atlanta & West Point road he became sick and was left by his master with a pass—the pass having been destroyed by being in the rain.

The owner will please come forward, prove property, pay expenses and take him away.

jan20–tf J. H. MOORE, Jailor.

Notice.

BROUGHT TO JAIL AT GREENVILLE, Meriwether county, Ga., a NEGRO MAN by the name of BILL, who from appearance, is about forty years of age, and says that he belongs to a man by the name of Faulkner, a negro trader: that he ran away from said Faulkner at West Point, Ga., about three years ago.

The owner is requested to come forward, prove property, pay charges and take him away, or he will be disposed of as the law directs.

dec9–tf JNO. S. BLALOCK, Sh'ff.

West Point Bulletin please copy.

Brought to the Jail

OF TROUP COUNTY, GEORGIA, on the 2d inst., a NEGRO MAN, who says his name is SAM, and belongs to Charles Snowden, near Brooklin, Conecuh county, Ala. He is 5 feet 4 inches high, rather light complected, with a flat nose, about 35 years old, weighs 150 pounds. Says he was working on the Atlanta & West Point Rail Road.

The owner will come forward, prove property, pay charges and take him away.

fa 10–tf J. H. MOORE, Jailor.

Thousands of slaves deserted their owners in what historian W.E.B. DuBois called a general strike against the Confederacy. And the closer the war came to its conclusion, the more slaves ran away as evidenced by these notices from the LaGrange Reporter *of March 3, 1865.*

majority of Georgians opposed it. What support the Confederacy did have eroded quickly as the passions of 1861 faded under the realities of war.

The government's conscription policy of 1862 only accelerated the decline of enthusiasm for the war. Most devastating to the cause of Southern independence were the attitudes of the planters and the privileges granted them by the government. Not only were they exempt from the draft but they continued to grow too much cotton while their poorer neighbors and Confederate soldiers went hungry. In doing so, planters literally starved the Confederacy out of existence. For those who had not already grasped the war's base reality, it became clear enough by 1862 that the struggle was little more than a

William Andrews of Clay County joined the army in February 1861 and served through the entire war. After the war Andrews moved to Dawson, Georgia, married Amanda Avent. He worked as a carpenter and farmer, and later a contractor. He and Amanda later lived in Atlanta, where she died sometime before 1888. Andrews finally settled in Gordon County and began drawing a veteran's pension in 1900. Nine years later he moved back to Atlanta to be near his children. He died in 1920 at age eighty-two. Courtesy of Mark Reynolds, Tucker, Georgia.

rich man's war. Few outside the slaveholding class could support actively the Confederacy once that realization set in. Some went so far as to take up arms against it. The war continued for three more years only because Lincoln had his own problems with popular support in the North.

Even among those who stuck with the Confederacy to its painful end, most did so half-heartedly. What loyalty they still felt was more for their commanders and comrades than the government in Richmond. William Andrews of Clay County had joined the army in February 1861 and remained through the entire war. Few could match his record of service to the cause of Southern independence. Still, in May of 1865 he wrote: "While it is a bitter pill to have to come back into the Union, don't think there is much regret for the loss of the Confederacy. The treatment the soldiers have received from the government in various ways put them against it."[150] That attitude on the part of Johnny Rebs throughout the ranks, brought on largely by class antagonism, was among the major reasons for Confederate defeat.

NOTES

1. *O.R.*, series 1, vol. 19, part 2, p. 622.

2. *Early County (Ga.) News*, April 5, 1865.

3. In his seminal study of the secession crisis, David Potter looked at the vote on secession throughout the South and concluded: "At no time during the winter of 1860–1861 was secession desired by a majority of the people of the slave states. . . . Furthermore, secession was not basically desired even by a majority in the lower South, and the secessionists succeeded less because of the intrinsic popularity of their program than because of the extreme skill with which they utilized an emergency psychology, the promptness with which they invoked unilateral action by individual states, and the firmness with which they refused to submit the question of secession to popular referenda." See David M. Potter, *Lincoln and His Party in the Secession Crisis* (New Haven, Conn.: Yale University Press, 1942), 208. Potter's conclusions are supported by Paul D. Escott's more recent study, *After Secession: Jefferson Davis and the Failure of Confederate Nationalism* (Baton Rouge: Louisiana State University Press, 1978), 23–28, 42–44.

4. A.P. Aldrich to James H. Hammond, November 25, 1860, in Lillian A. Kibler, "Unionist Sentiment in South Carolina," *Journal of Southern History* 4 (1938), 358.

5. Watkins, *Co. Aytch*, 69.

6. *Athens (Ga.) Southern Watchman*, September 28, 1864.

7. Stephen E. Ambrose, "Yeoman Discontent in the Confederacy," *Civil War History* 8 (1962): 263.

8. Hagan to Amanda Roberts Hagan, July 23, 1863, in Bell I. Wiley, ed., "The Confederate Letters of John W. Hagan," *Georgia Historical Quarterly* 38 (1954): 196.

9. *Atlanta (Ga.) Southern Confederacy*, October 25, 1862.

10. United States Census Bureau, Population of the United States in 1860.

11. Co-Operation Meeting of the Citizens of Stewart County, December 18, 1860, broadside in Stewart—Archives Folder, File 2, Counties, Georgia Department of Archives and History, Atlanta.

12. A. Hood to Cobb, December 19, 1860, in Ulrich B. Phillips, ed., *The Correspondence of Robert Toombs, Alexander H. Stephens, and Howell Cobb* (Washington, D.C.: Government Printing Office, 1913), 524.

13. Michael P. Johnson, *Toward a Patriarchal Republic: The Secession of Georgia* (Baton Rouge: Louisiana State University Press, 1977), 63.

14. *Journal of the Public and Secret Proceedings of the Convention of the People of Georgia, 1861* (Milledgeville: Boughton, Nisbet, and Barnes, 1861), 15–23, 31–40.

15. Donald L. Grant, *The Way it Was in the South: The Black Experience in Georgia*, edited, with introduction, by Jonathan Grant (New York: Birch Lane Press, 1993), 81.

16. Robert Toombs, *Speech on the Crisis Delivered Before the Georgia Legislature* (Washington, D.C.: Lemuel Towers, 1860). For the major arguments on secession by leading political figures in Georgia see William W. Freehling and Craig M. Simpson, eds., *Secession Debated: Georgia's Showdown in 1860* (New York: Oxford University Press, 1992).

17. *Thomaston (Ga.) Upson Pilot*, December 8, 1860.

18. T. Conn Bryan, *Confederate Georgia* (Athens: University of Georgia Press, 1953), 9.

19. R. D. Chapman, *A Georgia Soldier in the Civil War, 1861–1865* (Houston, Tex.: n.p., 1923), 6.

20. Some of these are suggested in Lewis N. Wynne and Guy Porcher Harrison, "'Plain Folk' Coping in the Confederacy: The Garrett-Asbell Letters," *Georgia Historical Quarterly* 72 (1988): 102.

21. Bryan, *Confederate Georgia*, 22; James A. Riley, "Desertion and Disloyalty in Georgia During the Civil War" (M. A. thesis, University of Georgia, 1951), 7.

22. Robert C. Black, III, "The Railroads of Georgia in the Confederate War Effort," *Journal of Southern History* 18 (1947): 517–18.

23. Coleman to Brown, September 13, 1861, Governor's Incoming Correspondence, 1861–1865, Georgia Department of Archives and History, Atlanta.

24. Georgia Lee Tatum, *Disloyalty in the Confederacy* (Chapel Hill: University of North Carolina Press, 1934), 73.

25. Andrew W. Cain, *History of Lumpkin County* (Atlanta: Stein Printing, 1932), 87.

26. Riley, "Desertion and Disloyalty," 3.

27. Charles Jewett Swift, *The Last Battle of the Civil War* (Columbus, Ga.: Gilbert Printing Co., 1915), 27.

28. Aiken to Brown, February 15, 1861, Talemon Cuyler Collection, University of Georgia, Athens.

29. Brown to A.I. Whitten, T.H. Callaway, and others, April 24, 1861, Governor's Letter Book, 1861–1865, Georgia Department of Archives and History, Atlanta; Johnson, *Toward a Patriarchal Republic*, 63–64.

30. Val L. McGee, *Claybank Memories: A History of Dale County, Alabama* (Ozark, Ala.: Dale County Historical Society, 1989), 42.

31. Crawford to Brown, July 31, 1861, Governor's Incoming Correspondence.

32. Escott, *After Secession*, 115.

33. *Early County News*, September 28, 1864.

34. Lamar to Cobb, November 3, 1861, Howell Cobb Papers, University of Georgia, Athens.

35. Mrs. A. E. Moore to Brown, October 7, 1862, Cuyler Collection.

36. Parthenia A. Hague, *A Blockaded Family: Life in Southern Alabama During the Civil War* (Cambridge, Mass.: Riverside Press, 1888), 101; Bryan, *Confederate Georgia*, 61; Diffee William Standard, *Columbus, Georgia, in the Confederacy: The Social and Industrial Life of the Chattahoochee River Port* (New York: William-Frederick Press, 1954), 47; John F. Reiger, "Deprivation, Disaffection, and Desertion in Confederate Florida," *Florida Historical Quarterly* 48 (1969–70): 280.

37. Standard, *Columbus in the Confederacy*, 46.

38. William Butler to Stephens, November 11, 1861, Alexander H. Stephens Papers, Library of Congress, Washington, D.C.

39. *Early County News*, December 2, 1863, January 13 and April 27, 1864.

40. Jordan to Brown, November 18, 1861, Governor's Incoming Correspondence.

41. *Early County News*, April 19, 1865.

42. Anonymous to Brown, n.d., Governor's Incoming Correspondence.

43. Mary Elizabeth Massey, *Ersatz in the Confederacy* (Columbia: University of South Carolina Press, 1952), 52; Bryan, *Confederate Georgia*, 60.

44. *Early County News*, January 20, 1864.

45. Bryan, *Confederate Georgia*, 57, 60–61.

46. Frederick Burtz to Brown, March 29, 1862, Governor's Incoming Correspondence. For commentary on the letter and the issue see Lee W. Formwalt, "Planters and Cotton Production as a Cause of Confederate Defeat: Evidence from Southwest Georgia," *Georgia Historical Quarterly* 74 (1990): 272–75.

47. Bryan, *Confederate Georgia*, 118.

48. Allen D. Candler, comp., *The Confederate Records of Georgia*, 6 vols. (Atlanta: State Printing Office, 1909–11), 2: 268–69; *Acts of the General Assembly of the State of Georgia, 1862* (Milledgeville: Boughton, Nisbet, and Barnes, 1862), 20–22.

49. Tatum, *Disloyalty in the Confederacy*, 19.

50. Bryan, *Confederate Georgia*, 122.

51. Stanley Lebergott, "Why the South Lost: Commercial Purpose in the Confederacy," *Journal of American History* 70 (1983): 69.

52. Ibid., 71–72.

53. John H. Jones and D. Dudley to Brown, March 5, 1862, Governor's Incoming Correspondence.

54. Ibid.

55. William A. Clarke to E. Cody, September 7, 1861, in Edmund Cody Burnett, ed., "Letters of Barnett Hardeman Cody and Others, 1861–1864," *Georgia Historical Quarterly* 23 (1939): 290.

56. *Early County News*, August 10, 1864.

57. Peter Wallenstein, *From Slave South to New South: Public Policy in Nineteenth-Century Georgia* (Chapel Hill: University of North Carolina Press, 1987), 120; Rebecca Christian, "Georgia and the Confederate Policy of Impressing Supplies," *Georgia Historical Quarterly* 28 (1944): 2.

58. *Early County News*, March 16, 1864.

59. J. B. Guest to Brown, May 20, 1862, Governor's Incoming Correspondence.

60. Cleveland to Brown, November 3, 1863, ibid.

61. *Early County News*, March 30, 1864.

62. Ibid., August 24, 1864.

63. Asbell to Asbell, November 1 and 19, 1863, Wynne and Harrison, "'Plain Folk' Coping in the Confederacy," 115, 117.

64. Petition from Women of Miller County, Georgia, to Secretary of War James Seddon and President Jefferson Davis, September 8, 1863, Letters Received, Confederate Secretary of War, National Archives, Washington, D.C.

65. *O.R.*, series 1, vol. 30, part 2, pp. 629–31, 635–36; Henderson, *Roster of the Confederate Soldiers of Georgia*, 5: 775–86.

66. Wayne Flynt, *Poor but Proud: Alabama's Poor Whites* (Tuscaloosa: University of Alabama Press, 1989), 41.

67. *Early County News*, January 25 and February 8, 1865; *Macon (Ga.) Telegraph*, February 24 and March 8, 1865; Nellie Cook Davis, *The History of Miller County, Georgia, 1856–1980* (Colquitt, Ga.: Colquitt Garden Club, 1980), 171, 395.

68. Barnsley to Thomas C. Gilmour, January 26 and December 31, 1862, Godfrey Barnsley Papers, University of Georgia, Athens.

69. Riley, "Desertion and Disloyalty," 33; *Atlanta Southern Confederacy*, March 20, 1863; *Americus (Ga.) Sumter Republican*, March 27, 1863; *Columbus (Ga.) Sun*, April 11, 1863, and April 22, 1864; *Augusta (Ga.) Chronicle and Sentinel*, April 24, 1864; *Augusta (Ga.) Constitutionalist*, April 23, 1864. For an in depth treatment of food riots in Georgia see Teresa Crisp Williams, "'The Women Rising': Class and Gender in Civil War Georgia" (M.A. thesis, Valdosta State University, 1999).

70. Louise Calhoun Barfield, *History of Harris County, Georgia, 1827–1961* (Columbus, Ga.: Columbus Office Supply Co., 1961), 758.

71. Brooks to husband, September 3, 1862, Confederate Letters, Georgia Department of Archives and History, Atlanta.

72. Watkins, *Co. Aytch*, 194.

73. J. Boyd to brother, February 16, 1862, Boyd Letters, Columbus State University, Columbus, Ga.

74. Curry to Duncan Curry, December 9, 1862, Curry Hill Plantation Records, Georgia Department of Archives and History, Atlanta.

75. Lovett to Lovett, March 26, 1862, Mills Lane, comp., *Times That Prove People's Principles: Civil War in Georgia—A Documentary History* (Savannah: Beehive Press, 1993), 97.

76. Lovett to Lovett, February 14, 1864, ibid., 105.

77. Asbell to wife Sarah Asbell, October 19 and November 19, 1863, Wynne and Harrison, "'Plain Folk' Coping in the Confederacy," 114, 116–17.

78. Geoffrey C. Ward, *The Civil War* (New York: Alfred Knopf, 1992), 201.

79. William H. Andrews, *Footprints of a Regiment: A Recollection of the First Georgia Regulars, 1861–1865* (Atlanta: Longstreet Press, 1992), 20.

80. Thurman to Brown, October 11, 1864, Governor's Incoming Correspondence.

81. Williams to Brown, June 20, 1864, ibid.

82. Mrs. S. E. Cook to Brown, August 16, 1864, ibid.

83. Watkins, *Co. Aytch*, 194.

84. Andrews, *Footprints of a Regiment*, 39.

85. Ibid.

86. John Joseph Kirkland, Compiled Service Records, National Archives, Washington, D.C.; Henderson, *Roster of the Confederate Soldiers of Georgia, 1861–1865*, 5: 372; Union Missionary Baptist Church Cemetery Records, Miller County, Georgia.

87. *Early County News*, May 4, 1864.

88. See David Carlson, "'The Distemper of the Time': Conscription, the Courts, and Planter Privilege in Civil War South Georgia," *Journal of Southwest Georgia History* 13 (1999): 1–21.

89. "Miss Abby's" Diary, January 20, 1864, University of Georgia, Athens.

90. George A. Mercer Diary, March 3, 1862, University of North Carolina, Chapel Hill.

91. Harden to his mother, April 17, 1862, Edward Harden Papers, Duke University, Durham, N.C.

92. Andrews, *Footprints of a Regiment*, 121–23.

93. Douglas Clare Purcell, "Military Conscription in Alabama During the Civil War," *Alabama Review* 34 (1981): 104.

94. Andrews, *Footprints of a Regiment*, 110.

95. *Early County News*, March 30, 1864.

96. Riley, "Desertion and Disloyalty," 84.

97. Emma J. Slade Prescott Reminiscences, Atlanta Historical Society Archives.

98. Bryan, *Confederate Georgia*, 90.

99. Bush to Brown, October 16, 1863, and Mrs. B. J. Smith to Brown, August 13, 1864, Governor's Incoming Correspondence.

100. Mary Grist Whitehead, ed., *Collections of Early County Historical Society*, 2 vols. Colquitt, Ga.: Automat Printers, 1971), 1: 134.

101. Riley, "Desertion and Disloyalty," 64.

102. Ibid., 75.

103. *O.R.*, series 1, vol. 49, part 1, p. 963.

104. *Augusta Constitutionalist*, June 24 and July 24, 1862; *Milledgeville (Ga.) Southern Union*, July 29, 1862.

105. *Augusta Constitutionalist*, July 26, 1862.

106. *American Annual Cyclopedia, 1862* (New York: D. Appleton, 1862), 16.

107. Cain, *History of Lumpkin County*, 158–64, 165–68.

108. *O.R.*, series 1, vol. 2, p. 786.

109. Kenneth C. Martis, *Historical Atlas of the Congresses of the Confederate States* (New York: Simon and Shuster, 1994), 87.

110. *Columbus Enquirer*, October 9, 1863; *Columbus Sun*, October 13, 1863.

111. *Columbus Enquirer*, October 9, 1863.

112. Richard Nelson Current, *Lincoln's Loyalists: Union Soldiers from the Confederacy* (New York: Oxford University Press, 1994), 218.

113. O'Connor to Brown, March 10, 1862, Governor's Incoming Correspondence.

114. Edward Mueller, *Perilous Journeys: A History of Steamboating on the Chattahoochee, Apalachicola, and Flint Rivers, 1828–1928* (Eufaula, Ala.: Historic Chattahoochee Commission, 1990), 109.

115. *Early County News*, January 20, 1864; Bessie Martin, *Desertion of Alabama Troops from the Confederate Army: A Study in Sectionalism* (New York: AMS Press, 1966), 52.

116. *O.R.*, series 1, vol. 28, part 2, p. 411.

117. *O.R.*, series 1, vol. 35, part 1, pp. 529–32; *O.R.*, series 1, vol. 36, part 2, pp. 551–52.

118. *O.R.*, series 4, vol. 3, pp. 1119–20.

119. W. R. Houghton and M. B. Houghton, *Two Boys in the Civil War and After* (Montgomery, Ala.: The Paragon Press, 1912), 237–41.

120. John W. Riley to Brown, July 22 (no year), Governor's Incoming Correspondence.

121. Riley, "Desertion and Disloyalty," 69.

122. *O.R.*, series 1, vol. 28, part 2, p. 273.

123. *Early County News*, February 10, 1864.

124. Ibid., February 24, 1864.

125. *O.R.*, series 1, vol. 38, part 4, p. 594.

126. *O.R.*, series. 1, vol. 44, p. 977.

127. *O.R.*, series 1, vol. 44, pp. 827–28.

128. Riley, "Desertion and Disloyalty," 64.

129. Maxine Turner, *Navy Gray: A Story of the Confederate Navy on the Chattahoochee and Apalachicola Rivers* (Tuscaloosa: University of Alabama Press, 1988), 130–31, 325 n. 6.

130. Ibid., 130.

131. [name illegible] to Brown, October 5, 1864, Governor's Incoming Correspondence.

132. *O.R.*, series 1, vol. 23, part 2, p. 738.

133. George M. Battey, Jr., *A History of Rome and Floyd County* (Atlanta: n.p., 1922), 197–99.

134. *Atlanta Southern Confederacy*, February 4, 1863.

135. G. W. Lee to Brown, June 12, 1863, Governor's Letter Book.

136. *Milledgeville (Ga.)Confederate Union*, November 24, 1863.

137. *Early County News*, March 30, 1864.

138. Ibid., October 5, 1864.

139. Citizens of Wilcox County to Brown, January 14, 1865, Joseph E. Brown Papers, University of Georgia, Athens; *O.R.*, series 1, vol. 47, part 2, p. 31.

140. *Early County News*, April 5, 1865.

141. Julia A. Brooks and others to Brown, June 22, 1864, Petitions to the Governor of Georgia, 1861–65, Georgia Department of Archives and History, Atlanta.

142. Chessy to Brown, October 7, 1864, Governor's Incoming Correspondence.

143. Sheffield to Brown, September 30, 1864, ibid.

144. Henry Cleveland, *Alexander H. Stephens in Public and Private with Letters and Speeches* (Philadelphia: National Publishing Company, 1866), 721.

145. *O.R.*, series 4, vol. 3, pp. 1009–10.

146. *Columbus Times*, February 15, 1865.

147. David Carlson, "Wiregrass Runners: Conscription, Desertion, and the Origins of Discontent in Civil War South Georgia" (M.A. thesis, Valdosta State University, 1999), 66; *Augusta Constitutionalist*, June 24, 1862; Christopher C. Meyers, "'The Wretch Vickery' and the Brooks County Civil War Slave Conspiracy," *Journal of Southwest Georgia History* 12 (1997): 27–38.

148. Clarence L. Mohr, *On the Threshold of Freedom: Masters and Slaves in Civil War Georgia* (Athens: University of Georgia Press, 1986), 283.

149. E. Merton Coulter, *The Confederate States of America, 1861–1865* (Baton Rouge: Louisiana State University Press, 1950), 105.

150. Andrews, *Footprints of a Regiment*, 184.

BIBLIOGRAPHY

Primary Sources

Archival Material, Manuscript Collections, and Cemetery Records

"Miss Abby's" Diary. University of Georgia, Athens.

Barnsley, Godfrey, Papers. University of Georgia, Athens.

Boyd Letters. Columbus State University, Columbus, Georgia.

Brown, Joseph E., Papers. University of Georgia, Athens.

Cobb, Howell, Papers. University of Georgia, Athens.

Confederate Letters. Georgia Department of Archives and History, Atlanta.

Co-Operation Meeting of the Citizens of Stewart County, December 18, 1860. Broadside in Stewart—Archives Folder, File 2, Counties, Georgia Department of Archives and History, Atlanta.

Curry Hill Plantation Records. Georgia Department of Archives and History, Atlanta.

Cuyler, Talemon, Collection. University of Georgia, Athens.

Davenport Papers. University of Georgia, Athens.

Davenport, Henry Thomas. Compiled Service Records. National Archives, Washington, D.C.

Governor's Incoming Correspondence, 1861–65. Georgia Department of Archives and History, Atlanta.

Governor's Letter Book, 1861–1865. Georgia Department of Archives and History, Atlanta.

Harden, Edward, Papers. Duke University, Durham, N.C.

Letters Recieved. Confederate Secretary of War. National Archives, Washington, D.C.

Kirkland, John Joseph. Compiled Service Records. National Archives, Washington, D.C.

Mercer, George A., Diary. University of North Carolina, Chapel Hill.

Petitions to the Governor of Georgia, 1861–65. Georgia Department of Archives and History, Atlanta.

Prescott, Emma J. Slade, Reminiscences. Atlanta Historical Society Archives.

Pryor, Shepard Green, Letters. University of Georgia, Athens.

Rushin Papers. Georgia Department of Archives and History, Atlanta.

Rushin, Thomas Jefferson. Compiled Service Records. National Archives, Washington, D.C.

Stephens, Alexander H., Papers. Library of Congress, Washington, D.C.

Union Missionary Baptist Church Cemetery Records. Miller County, Georgia.

Government Documents

Acts of the General Assembly of the State of Georgia, 1862. Milledgeville: Boughton, Nisbet, and Barnes, 1862.

Candler, Allen D., comp. *The Confederate Records of the State of Georgia.* 6 vols. (vol. 5 never published). Atlanta: State Printing Office, 1909–11.

Henderson, Lillian, comp. *Roster of the Confederate Soldiers of Georgia, 1861–1865.* 6 vols. Hapeville, Ga.: Longina and Porter, 1959–64.

Journal of the Public and Secret Proceedings of the Convention of the People of Georgia, 1861. Milledgeville: Boughton, Nisbet, and Barnes, 1861.

U.S. Census Bureau. Seventh Census of the United States, 1850.

_____. Population of the United States in 1860. Washington, D.C.: Robert Armstrong, 1853. Reprint, New York: Norman Ross, 1990

War of the Rebellion: A Compilation of the Official Records of the Union and Confederate Armies. 128 parts in 70 vols. and atlas. Washington, D.C.: Government Printing Office, 1880–1901.

Newpapers and Periodicals

Americus (Ga.) Sumter Republican

Atlanta (Ga.) Southern Confederacy

Athens (Ga.) Southern Watchman

Augusta (Ga.) Chronicle and Sentinel

Augusta (Ga.) Constitutionalist

Columbus (Ga.) Sun

Columbus (Ga.) Enquirer

Early County (Ga.) News

LaGrange (Ga.) Reporter

Macon (Ga.) Telegraph

Milledgeville (Ga.) Southern Union

Milledgeville (Ga.) Confederate Union

Harper's Weekly, (N.Y.)

Thomaston (Ga.) Upson Pilot

Published Letters, Papers, Seriels, Journals, and Memoirs

Alexander, E.P. *Military Memoirs of a Confederate*. New York: Charles Scribner's Sons, 1907.

American Annual Cyclopedia, 1862. New York: D. Appleton, 1862.

Americus City Directory, 1891–93. Americus, Georgia: The Americus Times Publishing Co., 1893.

Andrews, William H. *Footprints of a Regiment: A Recollection of the First Georgia Regulars, 1861–1865*. Atlanta: Longstreet Press, 1992.

Benson, Susan Williams, ed. *Berry Benson's Civil War Book*. Athens: University of Georgia Press, 1962.

Bernard, George S., ed. *War Talks of Confederate Veterans*. Petersburg, Va.: Fenn and Owen Publishers, 1892.

Blackford, W.W. *War Years with Jeb Stuart*. New York: Charles Scribner's Sons, 1945.

Borcke, Heros von. *Memoirs of the Confederate War for Independence*. 2 vols. New York: Peter Smith, 1938.

Buel, Clarence C., and Robert U. Johnson, eds. *Battles and Leaders of the Civil War*. 4 vols. New York: Century, 1887–88.

Burnett, Edmund Cody, ed. "Letters of Barnett Hardeman Cody and Others, 1861–1864." *Georgia Historical Quarterly* 23 (1939): 265–99, 362–80.

Chapman, R.D. *A Georgia Soldier in the Civil War, 1861–1865*. Houston, Tex.: n.p., 1923.

Cleveland, Henry. *Alexander H. Stephens in Public and Private with Letters and Speeches, Before, During, and Since the War*. Philadelphia: National Publishing Company, 1866.

Commager, Henry Steele, ed. *The Blue and the Gray: The Story of the Civil War as Told by Participants*. 2 vols. New York: Bobbs-Merill Co., 1950.

Crary, Catherine S., ed. *Dear Belle: Letters From a Cadet and Officer to His Sweetheart, 1858–65.* Middleton, Conn.: Wesleyan University Press, 1965.

Dinkins, James. *Personal Recollections and Experiences in the Confederate Army*. Cincinnati: Robert Clarke Company, 1897.

Dooley, John. *John Dooley: Confederate Soldier - His War Journal.* Edited by Joseph T. Durkin. Washington, D.C.: Georgetown University Press, 1945.

Douglas, Henry Kyd. *I Rode With Stonewall.* Chapel Hill: University of North Carolina Press, 1940.

Freehling, William W., and Craig M. Simpson, eds. *Secession Debated: Georgia's Showdown in 1860*. New York: Oxford University Press, 1992.

Hague, Parthenia A. *A Blockaded Family: Life in Southern Alabama During the Civil War*. Cambridge, Mass.: Riverside Press, 1888.

Haynes, Draughton S. *The Field Diary of a Confederate Soldier.* Darien, Ga.: The Ashantilly Press, 1963.

Hill, Benjamin H., Jr. *Senator Benjamin H. Hill of Georgia: His Life, Speeches and Writings.* Atlanta: H.C. Hudgins and Company, 1891.

Hopkins, Luther W. *From Bull Run to Appomattox: A Boy's View.* Baltimore, Md.: Fleet-McGinley, 1914.

Houghton, W. R. and M. B. Houghton. *Two Boys in the Civil War and After*. Montgomery, Ala.: The Paragon Press, 1912.

Johnson, Clifton, ed. *Battlefield Adventures: The Stories of Dwellers on the Scenes of Conflict*. Boston: Houghton Mifflin, 1915.

Lane, Mills, comp. *Times That Prove People's Principles: Civil War in Georgia—A Documentary History.* Savannah, Ga.: Beehive Press, 1993.

Long, A.L. *Memoirs of Robert E. Lee*. Secaucus, N.J.: Blue and Grey Press, 1983.

McClellan, H.B. *I Rode With Jeb Stuart.* Bloomington: Indiana University Press, 1958.

Merz, Louis. *Diary of Louis Merz.* Chattahoochee Valley Historical Society Bulletin Number 4, 1959.

Moses, Jacob Raphael. "A Southern Romantic." *Memoirs of American Jews, 1775–1865.* Jacob Rader Marcus, comp. Philadelphia: The Jewish Publication Society of America, 1955.

Neese, George M. *Three Years in the Confederate Horse Artillery.* New York: Neale Publishing, 1911.

Owen, W.M. *In Camp and Battle with the Washington Artillery of New Orleans.* Boston: Ticknor, 1885.

Phillips, Ulrich B., ed. *The Correspondence of Robert Toombs, Alexander H. Stephens, and Howell Cobb.* Washington, D.C.: Government Printing Office, 1913.

Sorrell, G. Moxley *Recollections of a Confederate Staff Officer.* Edited by Bell I. Wiley. Jackson, Tenn.: McCowat-Mercer Press, 1958.

Southern Historical Society Papers. 52 vols. Richmond, Va: 1876–1959.

Toombs, Robert. *Speech on the Crisis Delivered Before the Georgia Legislature.* Washington, D.C.: Lemuel Towers, 1860.

War Was the Place: A Centennial Collection of Confederate Soldier Letters. Chattahoochee Valley Historical Society Bulletin Number 5, 1961.

Watkins, Sam R. *Co. Aytch.* New York: Macmillian Publishing, 1962.

Wheeler, Richard, ed. *Voices of the Civil War.* New York: Thomas Y. Crowell Company, 1976.

Wiley, Bell Irvin, ed. "The Confederate Letters of John W. Hagan." *Georgia Historical Quarterly* 38 (1954): 170–200, 268–89.

Worsham, John H. *One of Jackson's Foot Cavalry.* New York: Neale Publishing, 1912.

Wynne, Lewis N. and Guy Porcher Harrison. "'Plain Folk' Coping in the Confederacy: The Garrett-Asbell Letters." *Georgia Historical Quarterly* 72 (1988): 102–118.

Secondary Sources

Ambrose, Stephen E. "Yeoman Discontent in the Confederacy." *Civil War History* 8 (1962): 259–68.

Andrews, J. Cutler. *The South Reports the Civil War*. Princeton, N.J.: Princeton University Press, 1970.

Barfield, Louise Calhoun. *History of Harris County, Georgia, 1827–1961*. Columbus, Ga.: Columbus Office Supply Co., 1961.

Battey, George M., Jr. *A History of Rome and Floyd County*. Atlanta, 1922.

Black, Robert C., III. "The Railroads of Georgia in the Confederate War Effort." *Journal of Southern History* 18 (1947): 511–34.

Brooks, Stewart. *Civil War Medicine*. Springfield, Ill.: Charles C. Thomas, Publisher, 1966.

Bryan, T. Conn. *Confederate Georgia*. Athens: University of Georgia Press, 1953.

Cain, Andrew W. *History of Lumpkin County*. Atlanta: Stein Printing, 1932.

Carlson, David. "'The Distemper of the Time': Conscription, the Courts, and Planter Privilege in Civil War South Georgia. *Journal of Southwest Georgia History* 13 (1998): 1–21.

_____. "Wiregrass Runners: Conscription, Desertion, and the Origins of Discontent in Civil War South Georgia." M.A. thesis, Valdosta State University, 1999.

Catton, Bruce C. *The Army of the Potomac*. 3 vols. Garden City, N.Y.: Doubleday, 1962.

Christian, Rebecca. "Georgia and the Confederate Policy of Impressing Supplies." *Georgia Historical Quarterly* 28 (1944): 1–33.

Coulter, E. Merton. *The Confederate States of America, 1861–1865.* Baton Rouge: Louisiana State University Press, 1950.

Cunningham, H.H. *Doctors in Gray*. Baton Rouge, Louisiana State University Press, 1958.

Current, Richard Nelson. *Lincoln's Loyalists: Union Soldiers from the Confederacy*. New York: Oxford University Press, 1994.

Davis, Nellie Cook. *The History of Miller County, Georgia, 1856–1980.* Colquitt, Ga.: Colquitt Garden Club, 1980.

Devens, Richard M. *The Pictoral Book of Anecdotes and Incidents of the War of the Rebellion*. Hartford, Conn.: Hartford Publishing Company, 1866.

Escott, Paul D. *After Secession: Jefferson Davis and the Failure of Confederate Nationalism*. Baton Rouge: Louisiana State University Press, 1978.

Flynt, Wayne. *Poor but Proud: Alabama's Poor Whites*. Tuscaloosa: University of Alabama Press, 1989.

Foote, Shelby. *The Civil War*. 3 vols. New York: Random House, 1974.

Formwalt, Lee W. "Planters and Cotton Production as a Cause of Confederate Defeat: Evidence from Southwest Georgia." *Georgia Historical Quarterly* 74 (1990): 269–76.

Frassanito, William A. *Antietam: The Photographic Legacy of America's Bloodiest Day*. New York: Charles Scribner's Sons, 1978.

Freeman, Douglas Southall. *Robert E. Lee*. 4 vols. New York: Charles Scribner's Sons, 1935.

______. *Lee's Lieuteants*. 3 vols. New York: Charles Scribner's Sons, 1944.

Grant, Donald L. *The Way it Was in the South: The Black Experience in Georgia*. Edited with introduction by Jonathan Grant. New York: Birch Lane Press, 1993.

Hattaway, Herman and Archer Jones. *How the North Won*. Chicago: University of Illinois Press, 1983.

Johnson, Michael P. *Toward a Patriarchal Republic: The Secession of Georgia*. Baton Rouge: Louisiana State University Press, 1977.

Johnson, Rossiter. *Campfire and Battlefield: A History of the Conflicts and Campaigns of the Great Civil War in the United States*. New York: Knight and Brown, 1896.

Kibler, Lillian A. "Unionist Sentiment in South Carolina in 1860." *Journal of Southern History* 4 (1938): 346–66.

Lebergott, Stanley. "Why the South Lost: Commercial Purpose in the Confederacy." *Journal of American History* 70 (1983): 58–74.

Livermore, Thomas L. *Numbers and Losses in the Civil War*. Bloomington: Indiana University Press, 1957.

Longstreet, Helen Dortch. *In the Path of Lee's Old War Horse*. Atlanta, Ga.: Caldwell Publishing, 1917.

Martin, Bessie. *Desertion of Alabama Troops From the Confederate Army: A Study in Sectionalism*. New York: AMS Press, 1966.

Martis, Kenneth C. *Historical Atlas of the Congresses of the Confederate States of America* New York: Simon and Schuster, 1994.

Massey, Mary Elizabeth. *Ersatz in the Confederacy*. Columbia: University of South Carolina Press, 1952.

McGee, Val L. *Claybank Memories: A History of Dale County, Alabama*. Ozark, Ala.: Dale County Historical Society, 1989.

Meyers, Christopher C. "'The Wretch Vickery' and the Brooks County Civil Ware Slave Conspiracy." *Journal of Southwest Georgia History* 12 (1997): 27–38.

Mohr, Clarence L. *On the Threshold of Freedom: Masters and Slaves in Civil War Georgia*. Athens: University of Georgia Press, 1986.

Mueller, Edward A. *Perilous Journeys: A History of Steamboating on the Chattahoochee, Apalachicola, and Flint Rivers, 1828–1928.* Eufaula, Ala.: Historic Chattahoochee Commission, 1990.

Murfin, James V. *The Gleam of Bayonets: The Battle of Antietam and the Maryland Campaign of 1862.* Baton Rouge: Louisiana State University Press, 1965.

Powell, Nettie. *History of Marion County, Georgia*. Columbus, Ga.: Historical Publishing, 1931.

Potter, David M. *Lincoln and His Party in the Secession Crisis*. New Haven, Conn.: Yale University Press, 1942.

Purcell, Douglas Clare. "Military Conscription in Alabama During the Civil War." *Alabama Review* 34 (1981): 94–106.

Reiger, John F. "Deprivation, Disaffection, and Desertion in Confederate Florida." *Florida Historical Quarterly* 48 (1969–70): 279–98.

Riley, James A. "Desertion and Disloyalty in Georgia During the Civil War." M.A. thesis, University of Georgia, 1951.

Sears, Stephen. *Landscape Turned Red: The Battle of Antietam*. New York: Tichnor and Fields, 1983.

Standard, Diffee William. *Columbus, Georgia, in the Confederacy: The Social and Industrial Life of the Chattahoochee River Port*. New York: William-Frederick Press, 1954.

Swift, Charles Jewett. *The Last Battle of the Civil War*. Columbus, Ga.: Gilbert Printing Co., 1915.

Tatum, Georgia Lee. *Disloyalty in the Confederacy*. Chapel Hill: University of North Carolina Press, 1934.

Thomas, Henry W. *History of the Doles-Cooke Brigade*. Atlanta, Ga.: Franklin Publishing, 1903.

Turner, Maxine. *Navy Gray: A Story of the Confederate Navy on the Chattahoochee and Apalachicola Rivers*. Tuscaloosa: University of Alabama Press, 1988.

Wallenstein, Peter. *From Slave South to New South: Public Policy in Nineteenth-Century Georgia.* Chapel Hill: University of North Carolina Press, 1987.

Ward, Geoffrey C. *The Civil War*. New York: Alfred Knopf, 1992.

Whitehead, Mary Grist, ed. *Collections of Early County Historical Society*. Vol. 1. Colquitt, Ga.: Automat Printers, 1971.

Wiley, Bell I. *Johnny Reb.* Baton Rouge: Louisiana State University Press, 1978.

Williams, Teresa Crisp, "'The Women Rising': Class and Gender in Civil War Georgia." M.A. thesis, Valdosta State University, 1999.

Williford, William. *Americus Through the Years*. Atlanta, Ga.: Cherokee Publishing, 1975.

INDEX